THE COMEDY OF ERRORS

By WILLIAM SHAKESPEARE

Preface and Annotations by
HENRY N. HUDSON

Introduction by
CHARLES HAROLD HERFORD

The Comedy of Errors
By William Shakespeare
Preface and Annotations by Henry N. Hudson
Introduction by Charles Harold Herford

Print ISBN 13: 978-1-4209-5555-2
eBook ISBN 13: 978-1-4209-5556-9

Cover Image: a detail of "Comedy of errors: two Dromios" by Henry Richter, c. 1829.

Please visit *www.digireads.com*

CONTENTS

INTRODUCTION 5

PREFACE.. 7

THE COMEDY OF ERRORS

DRAMATIS PERSONAE 9

ACT I.

SCENE I. 10
SCENE II. 14

ACT II.

SCENE I. 19
SCENE II. 22

ACT III.

SCENE I. 29

ACT IV.

SCENE I. 40
SCENE II. 43
SCENE III.. 46
SCENE IV. 49

ACT V.

SCENE I. 55

Introduction

The Comedy of Errors first appeared in the Folio of 1623, where it occupies the fifth place. Like *Love's Labour's Lost* it was mentioned among Shakespeare's comedies by Francis Meres in the *Palladis Tamia,* 1598. But it was undoubtedly composed several years before this, and there is no reason to suppose that, like *Love's Labour's Lost,* it underwent any revision. All its features of style, metre, characterisation, and structure point to the years 1589-91 as its date; and two explicit allusions confirm this view. Theobald first pointed out the reference in iii. 2. to the contemporary civil war in France. Dromio, describing the corpulent kitchen-maid to Antipholus, replies to the question in what part of her person he had found 'France,' in the words: 'In her forehead; armed and reverted, against her hair.' This is also applicable to the situation between 1589, when Henry III. appointed Henry IV. his successor, and 1593, when the civil war closed with Henry's actual recognition as King. The English expedition sent to his aid in 1591 marked the warm popular sympathy with his cause of which Shakespeare had already made use in *Love's Labour's Lost*; and the unflattering—in its more occult sense even ribald—allusion to France doubtless brought down the house. It is probable that a *Comedy of Errors* performed in 1594 'by the players' at Gray's Inn was Shakespeare's play. A *Historie of Error* (now lost) is recorded to have existed at a much earlier date—1st January 1577; but the wits and scholars who dictated intellectual fashions at the Inns of Court were not likely, at this moment of unparalleled dramatic advance, to revive an old play of the last decade but one.

To an audience of this type, Shakespeare's *Comedy of Errors* would peculiarly appeal by its obvious relation to two well-known plays of Plautus. Of one of these, the *Menæchmi,* an English version was published in 1595 by 'W. W.,' *i.e.* probably William Warner. The other plays translated by Warner remained in MS. But Shakespeare certainly imitated also—in a highly original way—a scene from the *Amphitruo*; and it is no violent hypothesis that the sometime scholar of Stratford grammar-school could and did read both in Latin. Plautus' *Menæchmi* is an amusing piece, of moderate merit. The Menæchmi are two brothers, one of whom (originally Sosicles) after the loss of the other is called by his name, and on growing up goes in search of him. They are distinguished in the English translation as Menæchmus 'the traveller' (T.) and 'the citizen' (C). The former has a servant Messenio. The scene is laid at Epidamnus (called in the English version *Epidamnum,* in the Folio Shakespeare *Epidamium*). Menæchmus C. arranges to dine with Erotium, a courtesan. Menæchmus T., who has just landed, is summoned to the dinner, and after eating it, is entrusted

with a cloak which Menæchmus C. has purloined from his wife for
Erotium, and a chain, her own property, to take to the dyer and the
goldsmith. Menæchmus C.'s wife ('Mulier') abuses him for the loss of
her cloak and sends him to claim it from Erotium. In the meantime she
meets Menæchmus T. with the cloak on his shoulders. Recriminations
ensue. She calls in her father ('Senex'), who mildly expostulates;
Menæchmus swears his innocence, is charged with madness, feigns
madness to scare them, and on their running off to fetch a physician,
flies to his ship. Returning they meet Menæchmus C, who is only saved
from forcible capture by the arrival of Menæchmus T.'s servant
Messenio. In reward he promises Messenio his freedom. Menæchmus
T. being 'reminded' of this promise angrily scouts it, but the dispute is
interrupted by the appearance of Menæchmus C. and the 'errors' are
cleared up.

In Shakespeare's hands this farcical plot lost nothing of its farcical
character. He even heightened the extravagance of the primary
supposition by doubling the pair of indistinguishable twins; but he
worked out the comical consequences of the situation with far greater
care than Plautus, touched its romantic possibilities with a lyrical
ardour to which Plautus was wholly strange, and set it in a framework
of tragedy of which the Plautine story contains no suggestion.

The central incident—the entertainment of the wrong Menæchmus
at dinner—was immensely improved with the aid of the motive already
referred to from Plautus' *Amphitruo.* Jupiter and Mercury there visit
Alcmena's house in the disguise of her husband Amphitruo and his
servant Sosia. After their departure the true Amphitruo and Sosia
arrive. It may well be that this suggested the introduction of the Dromio
twins, though Shakespeare gives still more piquancy to the idea by
making Antipholus and Dromio of Ephesus arrive at the door while
their counterparts of Syracuse are still within. This probably further
suggested the substitution of the wife for the courtesan, as the hostess
of Antipholus of Syracuse, Antipholus of Ephesus' visit to the
courtesan being made, with admirable tact, a not unnatural act of
vengeance for his apparent exclusion from his own house, instead of a
gratuitous infidelity, as it is in Plautus. The wife herself and her sister
are studied with a care and minuteness which the action certainly did
not require. In the change from Plautus' 'Mulier,' who rails at her
husband with only too good reason, to Shakespeare's Adriana, who
torments him with doubts at bed and board, and is ready to die in
despair at the loss of his love because he refuses to come home to
dinner, we see the change from pragmatical to psychological drama,
from the comedy of intrigue to the comedy of character, of which
otherwise there is not in this play very much. And Luciana brings us
altogether into the atmosphere of lyric love which pervades *The Two
Gentlemen* and the greater part of *A Midsummer-Night's Dream,* and is

half seriously disparaged in *Love's Labour's Lost.*

Still more significant is, finally, the story of Ægeon, which envelops the whole comic plot. It is probably Shakespeare's invention, and betrays the same instinct for accumulated effects and drastic contrasts. He had quadrupled the intricacies of the imbroglio by doubling the two lost Antipholuses with a second pair of twins; he quadruples the excitement of the final recovery by doubling them with a pair of lost parents, who at the same time recover their children and each other. And the foreboding of tragic harms which habitually overhangs for a while the early comedies, is here graver and more protracted than either in *A Midsummer-Night's Dream* or *The Two Gentlemen.* Valentine's banishment and Hermia's destination to a nunnery or death arouse no serious suspense; but Ægeon is a pathetic and moving figure, whose story—a masterpiece of Shakespeare's early narrative—strikes a note at the outset with which the subsequent action is in somewhat too marked dissonance for ripe art.

CHARLES HAROLD HERFORD

1901.

Preface

First printed in the folio of 1623. One of the twelve plays mentioned by Francis Meres in his *Palladis Tamia,* 1598. All are agreed in regarding it as among the Poet's earliest contributions to the stage; though it is somewhat uncertain whether, of the Comedies, *The Two Gentlemen of Verona* and the original form of *Lovers Labours Lost* may not have preceded it. In the *Gesta Grayorum,* 1594, we have the following: "After such sports, a *Comedy of Errors,* like to Plautus's *Menechmus,* was played by the players: so that night was begun, and continued to the end, in nothing but confusion and errors; whereupon it was ever afterwards called *The Night of Errors,*" This doubtless refers to the play in hand, and infers it to have been performed at Gray's-Inn in December, 1594. The date of the writing is further approximated from a curious piece of internal evidence. In iii. 2, Dromio of Syracuse, talking of the "kitchen wench" who made love to him, and who was "spherical like globe," so that he "could find out countries in her," in answer to the question, "Where France?" replies, "In her forehead; arm'd and reverted, making war against her hair." Here of course an equivoque was intended between *hair* and *heir,* else there were no apparent point in the jest; and the reference clearly is to the War of the League against Henry of Navarre, who became heir to the crown of France in 1589. As this war was on account of Henry's being a Protestant, the English people took great interest in it; in fact, Queen Elizabeth sent several bodies of troops to aid him; so that the allusion would naturally be understood and relished. The war, however, continued several years, until at length Henry embraced the Roman Catholic religion at St. Denis, in July, 1593.

The general idea or plan of the piece is borrowed from the *Menæchmi* of Plautus, but the plot is entirely recast, and made much more diverting by the variety and quick succession of the incidents. To the twin brothers of Plautus are added twin servants; which, to be sure, greatly heightens the improbability; but, as Schlegel observes, "when once we have lent ourselves to the first, which certainly borders on the incredible, we should not probably be disposed to cavil about the second; and if the spectator is to be entertained with mere perplexities, they cannot be too much varied."

There has been considerable diversity of opinion as to the *immediate* source of the plot. Collier discovered that an old drama entitled *The History of Error* was acted at Hampton Court, January 1, 1577, and probably again at Windsor on Twelfth Night, 1583; and he conjectures the Poet to have taken this as the basis of his comedy, and to have interwoven parts of it with his own matter, especially the doggerel verses. The older play not having been recovered, nor any part of it, we have no means of either refuting or verifying this conjecture.—Another opinion supposes the Poet to have drawn from a free version of the *Menæchmi* published in 1595, as "A pleasant and fine-conceited Comedy, taken out of the most excellent witty poet Plautus." This version, to be sure, did not come out till after *The Comedy of Errors* was written: but then Shakespeare may have seen it in manuscript; for in his preface the translator speaks of having "divers of this poet's comedies Englished, for the use and delight of private friends, who in Plautus's own words are not able to understand them." Nevertheless I am far from thinking this to have been the case; there being no such verbal or other resemblances between the two, as, in that case, could scarce have been avoided. The accurate Ritson ascertained that of this version not a single peculiar name or phrase or thought is to be traced in Shakespeare's comedy. On the whole, I cannot discover the slightest objection to supposing, along with Knight and Verplanck, that the Poet may have drawn directly from Plautus himself; the matter common to them both not being such but that it may well enough have been taken by one who had "small Latin."

HENRY N. HUDSON

1881.

The Comedy of Errors

DRAMATIS PERSONAE

SOLINUS, *Duke of Ephesus.*
ÆGEON, *a Merchant of Syracuse.*
ANTIPHOLUS OF EPHESUS, *Twin Son to Ægeon and Æmilia.*
ANTIPHOLUS OF SYRACUSE, *Twin Son to Ægeon and Æmilia.*
DROMIO OF EPHESUS, *twin Brother, Servant to the two Former.*
DROMIO OF SYRACUSE, *twin Brother, Servant to the two Former.*
BALTHAZAR, *a Merchant.*
ANGELO, *a Goldsmith.*
FIRST MERCHANT, *friend to Antipholus of Syracuse.*
SECOND MERCHANT, *to whom Angelo is a debtor.*
PINCH, *a Schoolmaster.*

ÆMILIA, *Wife to Ægeon, an Abbess at Ephesus.*
ADRIANA, *Wife to Antipholus of Ephesus.*
LUCIANA, *her Sister.*
LUCE, *Servant to Adriana.*
A COURTEZAN

Jailer, Officers, Attendants.

SCENE: *Ephesus*

ACT I.

SCENE I.

A Hall in DUKE'*s Palace.*

[*Enter the* DUKE, ÆGEON, JAILER, OFFICERS, *and other* ATTENDANTS.]

ÆGEON. Proceed, Solinus, to procure my fall
    And by the doom of death end woes and all.
DUKE SOLINUS. Merchant of Syracuse, plead no more;
    I am not partial to infringe[1] our laws:
    The enmity and discord which of late
    Sprung from the rancorous outrage of your duke
    To merchants, our well-dealing countrymen,—
    Who wanting guilders[2] to redeem their lives
    Have seal'd his rigorous statutes with their bloods,—
    Excludes all pity from our threatening looks.
    For, since the mortal[3] and intestine jars
    'Twixt thy seditious countrymen and us,
    It hath in solemn synods been decreed
    Both by the Syracusians and ourselves,
    To admit no traffic to our adverse towns
    Nay, more, if any born at Ephesus be seen
    At any Syracusian marts and fairs;
    Again: if any Syracusian born
    Come to the bay of Ephesus, he dies,
    His goods confiscate to the duke's dispose;[4]
    Unless a thousand marks be levied,
    To quit[5] the penalty and to ransom him.
    Thy substance, valued at the highest rate,
    Cannot amount unto a hundred marks;

---

[1] We should say, "I am not *the party* to infringe," or, "I'll *take no part* in infringing." So, in *Measure for Measure*, v. 1, we have "In this I'll be *impartial*"; meaning "I'll *take no part in* this."

[2] *Guelder* is the name of a Flemish and of a German coin; the former equal to about thirty-eight cents of our reckoning, the latter to about eighty-seven.

[3] *Mortal* is *deadly* or *fatal.* Commonly so in Shakespeare.

[4] *Dispose* for *disposal* or *disposition.* The Poet has many such shortened forms. So, in iii. 1, of this play we have "within the compass of *suspect*"; that is, *suspicion.*— *Confiscate*, also, for *confiscated.* The Poet has many like shortened preterites, such as *consecrate, dedicate, suffocate, situate,* and *contaminate.*

[5] To *quit*, here, is to *set free from*, or to *release;* much the same as to *acquit.* The Poet has it repeatedly so.

Therefore by law thou art condemned to die.
ÆGEON. Yet this my comfort: when your words are done,
    My woes end likewise with the evening sun.
DUKE SOLINUS. Well, Syracusian, say in brief the cause
    Why thou departed'st from thy native home
    And for what cause thou camest to Ephesus.
ÆGEON. A heavier task could not have been imposed
    Than I to speak my griefs unspeakable:
    Yet, that the world may witness that my end
    Was wrought by nature,[6] not by vile offence,
    I'll utter what my sorrows give me leave.
    In Syracusa was I born, and wed
    Unto a woman, happy but for me,
    And by me, had not our hap been bad.
    With her I lived in joy; our wealth increased
    By prosperous voyages I often made
    To Epidamnum; till my factor's death
    And the great care of goods at random left
    Drew me from kind embracements of my spouse:
    From whom my absence was not six months old
    Before herself—almost at fainting under
    The pleasing punishment that women bear—
    Had made provision for her following me
    And soon and safe arrived where I was.
    There had she not been long, but she became
    A joyful mother of two goodly sons;
    And, which was strange, the one so like the other,
    As[7] could not be distinguish'd but by names.
    That very hour, and in the self-same inn,
    A meaner woman was delivered
    Of such a burden, male twins, both alike:
    Those, for[8] their parents were exceeding poor,—
    I bought and brought up to attend my sons.
    My wife, not meanly proud of two such boys,
    Made daily motions for our home return:
    Unwilling I agreed. Alas! too soon,
    We came aboard!
    A league from Epidamnum had we sail'd,
    Before the always wind-obeying deep
    Gave any tragic instance[9] of our harm:

---

[6] Here, as in many other places, *nature* is *natural affection.*
[7] *As* is here equivalent to *that they.* The word was used much loosely in the Poet's time than it is now.
[8] *For in* the sense of *because* or *for that.* A frequent usage.
[9] Shakespeare uses *instance* with various shades of meaning not always easily

But longer did we not retain much hope;
For what obscured light the heavens did grant
Did but convey unto our fearful minds
A doubtful warrant of immediate death;
Which though myself would gladly have embraced,
Yet the incessant weepings of my wife,
Weeping before for what she saw must come,
And piteous plainings of the pretty babes,
That mourn'd for fashion, ignorant what to fear,
Forced me to seek delays for them and me.
And this it was,—for other means was none:—
The sailors sought for safety by our boat,
And left the ship, then sinking-ripe, to us:
My wife, more careful for the latter-born,
Had fasten'd him unto a small spare mast,
Such as seafaring men provide for storms;
To him one of the other twins was bound,
Whilst I had been like heedful of the other:
The children thus disposed, my wife and I,
Fixing our eyes on whom our care was fix'd,
Fasten'd ourselves at either end the mast;
And floating straight, obedient to the stream,
Were carried towards[10] Corinth, as we thought.
At length the sun, gazing upon the earth,
Dispersed those vapours that offended us;
And by the benefit of his wished light,
The seas wax'd calm, and we discovered
Two ships from far making amain[11] to us,
Of Corinth that, of Epidaurus this:
But ere they came,—O, let me say no more!
Gather the sequel by that went before.
DUKE SOLINUS. Nay, forward, old man; do not break off so;
    For we may pity, though not pardon thee.
ÆGEON. O, had the gods done so, I had not now
    Worthily term'd them merciless to us!
    For, ere the ships could meet by twice five leagues,
    We were encountered by a mighty rock;
    Which being violently borne upon,

---

distinguishable; such as *example, motive, ground, assurance, prognostic,* or *warning;* which latter is the meaning here.

[10] *Towards* is one or two syllables, and has the accent on the first or second syllabic, indifferently in Shakespeare, according to the needs of his verse. Here it is two syllables, with the accent on the first.

[11] *Amain* is *with strength,* or *strongly;* that is, *swiftly.* So, in Shakespeare, the adjective *main* often means *great* or *mighty,* as in the phrase, "with *main* strength."

Our helpful ship was splitted in the midst;
So that, in this unjust divorce of us,
Fortune had left to both of us alike
What to delight in, what to sorrow for.
Her part, poor soul! seeming as burdened
With lesser weight but not with lesser woe,
Was carried with more speed before the wind;
And in our sight they three were taken up
By fishermen of Corinth, as we thought.
At length, another ship had seized on us;
And, knowing whom it was their hap to save,
Gave healthful welcome to their shipwreck'd guests;
And would have reft the fishers of their prey,
Had not their bark been very slow of sail;
And therefore homeward did they bend their course.
Thus have you heard me sever'd from my bliss;
That by misfortunes was my life prolong'd,
To tell sad stories of my own mishaps.

DUKE SOLINUS. And for the sake of them thou sorrowest for,
Do me the favour to dilate at full
What hath befall'n of them and thee till now.

ÆGEON. My youngest boy, and yet my eldest care,
At eighteen years became inquisitive
After his brother: and importuned me
That his attendant—so his case was like,
Reft of his brother, but retain'd[12] his name—
Might bear him company in the quest of him:
Whom whilst I labour'd of a love[13] to see,
I hazarded the loss of whom I loved.
Five summers have I spent in furthest Greece,
Roaming clean[14] through the bounds of Asia,
And, coasting homeward, came to Ephesus;
Hopeless to find, yet loath to leave unsought
Or that or[15] any place that harbours men.
But here must end the story of my life;
And happy were I in my timely death,
Could all my travels warrant me they live.

DUKE SOLINUS. Hapless Ægeon, whom the fates have mark'd
To bear the extremity of dire mishap!

---

[12] The language, expressed in full, would *be* "*He was* reft of his brother, but retain'd." The Poet has many like ellipses.

[13] Here *of* stands for the relation of cause: *from* or *out of* a love.

[14] *Clean* is *utterly* or *entirely.* So in *Julius Cæsar,* i. 3: "Men may construe things *clean* from the purpose." Also in the 77th Psalm: "Is His mercy *clean* gone for ever?"

[15] *Or—or for either—aria* frequent in all English poetry.

Now, trust me, were it not against our laws,
Against my crown, my oath, my dignity,
Which princes, would they, may not disannul,[16]—
My soul would sue as advocate for thee.
But, though thou art adjudged to the death
And passed sentence may not be recall'd
But to our honour's great disparagement,
Yet I will favour thee in what I can.
Therefore, merchant, I'll limit thee this day
To seek thy life by beneficial help:[17]
Try all the friends thou hast in Ephesus;
Beg thou, or borrow, to make up the sum,
And live; if no, then thou art doom'd to die.—
Jailer, take him to thy custody.
JAILER. I will, my lord.
ÆGEON. Hopeless and helpless doth Ægeon wend,
But to procrastinate his lifeless end. [*Exeunt.*]

SCENE II.

The Mart.

[*Enter* ANTIPHOLUS *of Syracuse,* DROMIO *of Syracuse, and First* MERCHANT.]

FIRST MERCHANT. Therefore give out you are of Epidamnum,
Lest that[18] your goods too soon be confiscate.
This very day a Syracusian merchant
Is apprehended for arrival here;
And not being able to buy out his life
According to the statute of the town,
Dies ere the weary sun set in the west.
There is your money that I had to keep.
ANTIPHOLUS OF SYRACUSE. Go bear it to the Centaur, where we host,[19]
And stay there, Dromio, till I come to thee.
Within this hour it will be dinner-time:

---

[16] *Disannul* for *annul*, though properly meaning just the opposite. So in *Galatians*, iii. 17: "The covenant, that was confirmed before, the law cannot *disannul*."

[17] The Poet repeatedly uses *beneficial* for *beneficent* or *benevolent.* So that "beneficial help" is assistance rendered *out of charity* or *kindness.*

[18] "Lest *that*" is old language for *lest* simply. So we have if *that*, since *that*, though *that*, when *that*, &c., where we should now use only *if, since, though, when, &c.*

[19] To *host* for to *lodge.* So again in *All's Well*, iii. 5: "Come, pilgrim, I will bring you where you shall *host.*" In *King Lear*, v. 2, the word occurs as a substantive for *lodging.*—*Centaur* is the name of an inn. And so with *Phœnix* a little further on.

Till that, I'll view the manners of the town,
Peruse[20] the traders, gaze upon the buildings,
And then return and sleep within mine inn,
For with long travel I am stiff and weary.
Get thee away.
DROMIO OF SYRACUSE. Many a man would take you at your word,
And go indeed, having so good a mean.[21] [*Exit.*]
ANTIPHOLUS OF SYRACUSE. A trusty villain, sir, that very oft,
When I am dull with care and melancholy,
Lightens my humour with his merry jests.
What, will you walk with me about the town,
And then go to my inn and dine with me?
FIRST MERCHANT. I am invited, sir, to certain merchants,
Of whom I hope to make much benefit;
I crave your pardon. Soon at[22] five o'clock,
Please you, I'll meet with you upon the mart
And afterward consort[23] you till bed-time:
My present business calls me from you now.
ANTIPHOLUS OF SYRACUSE. Farewell till then: I will go lose
myself
And wander up and down to view the city.
FIRST MERCHANT. Sir, I commend you to your own content. [*Exit.*]
ANTIPHOLUS OF SYRACUSE. He that commends me to mine own
content
Commends me to the thing I cannot get.
I to the world am like a drop of water
That in the ocean seeks another drop,
Who, falling there to find his fellow forth,
Unseen, inquisitive, confounds[24] himself:
So I, to find a mother and a brother,
In quest of them, unhappy, lose myself.
Here comes the almanac of my true date.[25]—

[*Enter* DROMIO *of Ephesus.*]

---

[20] The Poet often has *peruse* for *mark* or *observe closely.* So in *Hamlet*, iv. 4: "He, being remiss, most generous, and free from all contriving, will not *peruse* the foils."

[21] *Mean* and *means* were used indifferently. Here *mean* refers to the money. And the sense is, "Many a man, having such a *purse of money* in trust, would *run away.*"

[22] *Soon at* is an old phrase for *about.* So again in iii. 1, of this play: "And *soon at* supper-time I'll visit you." Also in *The Merchant*, ii. 3: "*Soon at* supper shalt thou see Lorenzo."

[23] *Consort* for *accompany* or *attend.* So in *Love's Labours Lost*, ii. 1: "Sweet health and fair desires *consort* your Grace!"

[24] To *spend*, to *consume*, to *destroy* are old meanings of to *confound.—Forth* was often used with the sense of *out.*

[25] The almanac of his true date, because they were both born the same day.

What now? how chance thou art return'd so soon?

DROMIO OF EPHESUS. Return'd so soon! rather approach'd too late:
    The capon burns, the pig falls from the spit;[26]
    The clock hath strucken twelve upon the bell,—
    My mistress made it one upon my cheek:
    She is so hot because the meat is cold;
    The meat is cold because you come not home;
    You come not home because you have no stomach;[27]
    You have no stomach having broke your fast;
    But we that know what 'tis to fast and pray
    Are penitent for your default to-day.

ANTIPHOLUS OF SYRACUSE. Stop in your wind, sir: tell me this, I
        pray,—
    Where have you left the money that I gave you?

DROMIO OF EPHESUS. O,—sixpence, that I had o' Wednesday last
    To pay the saddler for my mistress' crupper?
    The saddler had it, sir; I kept it not.

ANTIPHOLUS OF SYRACUSE. I am not in a sportive humour now:
    Tell me, and dally not, where is the money?
    We being strangers here, how darest thou trust
    So great a charge from thine own custody?

DROMIO OF EPHESUS. I pray you, air, as you sit at dinner:
    I from my mistress come to you in post;[28]
    If I return, I shall be post indeed,
    For she will score[29] your fault upon my pate.
    Methinks your maw, like mine, should be your clock,
    And strike you home without a messenger.

ANTIPHOLUS OF SYRACUSE. Come, Dromio, come, these jests are
        out of season;
    Reserve them till a merrier hour than this.
    Where is the gold I gave in charge to thee?

DROMIO OF EPHESUS. To me, sir? why, you gave no gold to me.

ANTIPHOLUS OF SYRACUSE. Come on, sir knave, have done your
        foolishness,
    And tell me how thou hast disposed thy charge.

DROMIO OF EPHESUS. My charge was but to fetch you from the

---

[26] A *spit* was an iron rod, to thrust through a fowl, a pig, or a piece of meat, for roasting. The fowl or pig was then placed before the fire, so as to be kept turning; and the one who turned it was called a *turnspit.*

[27] *Stomach* for *appetite.* A frequent usage. Sometimes it means *courage;* that is, an appetite for fighting.

[28] "In *post*" is in *haste;* going with the speed of a postman.

[29] To *score*, as the word is here used, is to *mark;* as accounts were formerly kept by marking the items on a board or a post, or by cutting notches in a stick.—*Maw*, in the next line, is *stomach.*

mart

Home to your house, the Phoenix, sir, to dinner:

My mistress and her sister stays for you.

ANTIPHOLUS OF SYRACUSE. Now, as I am a Christian, answer me,

In what safe place you have bestow'd my money,

Or I shall break that merry sconce[30] of yours

That stands on tricks when I am undisposed:

Where is the thousand marks thou hadst of me?

DROMIO OF EPHESUS. I have some marks of yours upon my pate,

Some of my mistress' marks[31] upon my shoulders,

But not a thousand marks between you both.

If I should pay your Worship[32] those again,

Perchance you will not bear them patiently.

ANTIPHOLUS OF SYRACUSE. Thy mistress' marks? what mistress, slave, hast thou?

DROMIO OF EPHESUS. Your worship's wife, my mistress at the Phoenix;

She that doth fast till you come home to dinner,

And prays that you will hie you home to dinner.

ANTIPHOLUS OF SYRACUSE. What, wilt thou flout me thus unto my face,

Being forbid? There, take you that, sir knave. [*Beating him.*]

DROMIO OF EPHESUS. What mean you, sir? for God's sake, hold your hands!

Nay, and you will not, sir, I'll take my heels. [*Exit.*]

ANTIPHOLUS OF SYRACUSE. Upon my life, by some device or other

The villain is o'er-raught[33] of all my money.

They say this town is full of cozenage,

As, nimble jugglers that deceive the eye,

Dark-working sorcerers that change the mind,

Soul-killing witches that deform the body,

Disguised cheaters, prating mountebanks,

And many such-like liberties of sin:[34]

---

[30] *Sconce* is properly a round fortification; and, from the shape of the thing, the word came to be used of the *head.*

[31] A quibble between *mark* as a denomination of value, and *mark* in the ordinary sense. The English mark was equal to 13*s.* 8*d.,* or about $3.25.

[32] "Your *Worship*" was in common use as a phrase of deference, meaning somewhat less than "your *Honour.*"

[33] *O'er-raught* is an old form of *o'er-reached;* here meaning *cheated* or *defrauded.* To *cozen* had the same meaning; hence *cozenage.—Villain* and *knave* arc used here in the old English sense of *servant* or *thrall.*

[34] "Such-like *liberties of sin*" probably means "such-like *persons of sinful liberty*" or of *wicked license.—*A *mountebank* is what we call a *quack;* literally one who mounts a bank or a bench, and brags of his wares or of his skill.

If it prove so, I will be gone the sooner.
I'll to the Centaur, to go seek this slave:
I greatly fear my money is not safe. [*Exit.*]

ACT II.

SCENE I.

Before the House of ANTIPHOLUS *of Ephesus.*

[*Enter* ADRIANA *and* LUCIANA.]

ADRIANA. Neither my husband nor the slave return'd,
    That in such haste I sent to seek his master!
    Sure, Luciana, it is two o'clock.
LUCIANA. Perhaps some merchant hath invited him,
    And from the mart he's somewhere gone to dinner.
    Good sister, let us dine and never fret:
    A man is master of his liberty:
    Time is their master, and, when they see time,
    They'll go or come: if so, be patient, sister.
ADRIANA. Why should their liberty than ours be more?
LUCIANA. Because their business still lies out o' door.
ADRIANA. Look, when I serve him so, he takes it ill.
LUCIANA. O, know he is the bridle of your will.
ADRIANA. There's none but asses will be bridled so.
LUCIANA. Why, headstrong liberty is lash'd with woe.
    There's nothing situate under Heaven's eye
    But hath his[35] bound, in earth, in sea, in sky:
    The beasts, the fishes, and the winged fowls,
    Are their males' subjects and at their controls:
    Men, more divine, the masters of all these,
    Lords of the wide world and wild watery seas,
    Indued with intellectual sense and souls,
    Of more preeminence than fish and fowls,
    Are masters to their females, and their lords:
    Then let your will attend on their accords.
ADRIANA. This servitude makes you to keep unwed.
LUCIANA. Not this, but troubles of the marriage-bed.
ADRIANA. But, were you wedded, you would bear some sway.
LUCIANA. Ere I learn love, I'll practise to obey.
ADRIANA. How if your husband start some other hare?[36]

---

[35] *His* for *its*, the latter not being then an admitted word. Continually so in the Bible; as, "if the salt have lost *his* savour," and, "giveth to every seed *his* own body." In fact, *its* does not once occur in the Bible as printed in 1611.

[36] Meaning, probably, "fly off after some other woman." So in *As You Like It*, iv. 3: "Her love is not the *hare* that I do hunt." Also in *King Henry the Fourth, Part 1*, i. 3: "The blood more stirs, to rouse a lion than to *start a hare*."

LUCIANA. Till he come home again, I would forbear.
ADRIANA. Patience unmoved! no marvel though she pause;[37]
  They can be meek that have no other cause.[38]
  A wretched soul, bruised with adversity,
  We bid be quiet when we hear it cry;
  But were we burdened with like weight of pain,
  As much or more would we ourselves complain:
  So thou, that hast no unkind mate to grieve thee,
  With urging helpless[39] patience wouldst relieve me,
  But, if thou live to see like right bereft,
  This fool-begg'd patience[40] in thee will be left.
LUCIANA. Well, I will marry one day, but to try.
  Here comes your man; now is your husband nigh.

  [*Enter* DROMIO *of Ephesus.*]

ADRIANA. Say, is your tardy master now at hand?
DROMIO OF EPHESUS. Nay, he's at two hands with me, and that my
  two ears can witness.
ADRIANA. Say, didst thou speak with him? know'st thou his mind?
DROMIO OF EPHESUS. Ay, ay, he told his mind upon mine ear:
  Beshrew his hand, I scarce could understand it.[41]
LUCIANA. Spake he so doubtfully, thou couldst not feel his meaning?
DROMIO OF EPHESUS. Nay, he struck so plainly, I could too well
  feel his blows; and withal so doubtfully that I could scarce
  understand them.
ADRIANA. But say, I prithee, is he coming home?
  It seems he hath great care to please his wife.
DROMIO OF EPHESUS. Why, mistress, sure my master is horn-mad.
ADRIANA. Horn-mad, thou villain!
DROMIO OF EPHESUS. I mean not cuckold-mad;
  But, sure, he is stark mad.
  When I desired him to come home to dinner,
  He ask'd me for a thousand marks in gold:
  '*Tis dinner-time*, quoth I; *My gold*! quoth he;
  Your meat doth burn, quoth I; *My gold*! quoth he:

---

[37] Meaning, I suppose, that it is no wonder if patience keeps *quiet when* she has nothing to fret or disturb her.

[38] "No other cause" here means, apparently, "no cause to be otherwise."

[39] *Helpless* for *unhelping*. The Poet has it repeatedly thus. So in *Lucrece:* "This *helpless* smoke of words doth me no right."

[40] A *fool-begged* patience is a patience so nearly idiotic as to cause the subject of it to be "begged for a fool"; alluding to the old custom of soliciting the guardianship of fools or idiots with a view to get the management of their funds.

[41] A quibble between *understand* and *stand under*. So, in *The Two Gentlemen*, ii. 5, Launce says, "Why, *stand-under* and *understand* is all one."

Will you come home? quoth I; *My gold!* quoth he.
Where is the thousand marks I gave thee, villain?
The pig, quoth I, *is burn'd; My gold!* quoth he:
My mistress, sir, quoth I; *Hang up thy mistress!*
I know not thy mistress; out on thy mistress!
LUCIANA. Quoth who?
DROMIO OF EPHESUS. Quoth my master:
  'I know,' quoth he, 'no house, no wife, no mistress.'
  So that my errand, due unto my tongue,
  I thank him, I bare home upon my shoulders;
  For, in conclusion, he did beat me there.
ADRIANA. Go back again, thou slave, and fetch him home.
DROMIO OF EPHESUS. Go back again, and be new beaten home?
  For God's sake, send some other messenger.
ADRIANA. Back, slave, or I will break thy pate across.
DROMIO OF EPHESUS. And he will bless that cross with other
      beating:
  Between you I shall have a holy head.
ADRIANA. Hence, prating peasant! fetch thy master home.
DROMIO OF EPHESUS. Am I so round[42] with you as you with me,
  That like a football you do spurn me thus?
  You spurn me hence, and he will spurn me hither:
  If I last in this service, you must case me in leather. [*Exit.*]
LUCIANA. Fie, how impatience loureth in your face!
ADRIANA. His company must do his minions grace,
  Whilst I at home starve for a merry look.
  Hath homely age the alluring beauty took
  From my poor cheek? then he hath wasted it:
  Are my discourses dull? barren my wit?
  If voluble and sharp discourse be marr'd,
  Unkindness blunts it more than marble hard:
  Do their gay vestments his affections bait?
  That's not my fault,—he's master of my state:[43]
  What ruins are in me that can be found,
  By him not ruin'd? then is he the ground
  Of my defeatures. My decayed fair[44]
  A sunny look of his would soon repair
  But, too unruly deer, he breaks the pale
  And feeds from home; poor I am but his stale.[45]

---

[42] *Round* was much used for *plain-spoken;* hence the quibble here.

[43] *State* for *estate;* a common usage in the Poet's time.

[44] *Fair* is here used as a substantive, for *beauty.* Repeatedly so.—*Defeatures* is *change of features* or *disfigurement.*

[45] It appears that *stale* was sometimes used for *stalking-horse,* that is, a horse painted on stretched canvas, which the hunter carried before him in order to deceive the

LUCIANA. Self-harming jealousy,—fie, beat it hence!
ADRIANA. Unfeeling fools can with such wrongs dispense.[46]
    I know his eye doth homage otherwhere,
    Or else what lets[47] it but he would be here?
    Sister, you know he promised me a chain;—
    Would that alone, alone[48] he would detain,
    So he would keep fair quarter with his bed!
    I see the jewel best enamelled
    Will lose his beauty; yet the gold bides still,
    That others touch, and often touching will
    Wear gold: and no man that hath a name,
    By falsehood and corruption doth it shame.
    Since that my beauty cannot please his eye,
    I'll weep what's left away, and weeping die.
LUCIANA. How many fond fools serve mad jealousy! [*Exeunt.*]

SCENE II.

The Mart.

[*Enter* ANTIPHOLUS *of Syracuse.*]

ANTIPHOLUS OF SYRACUSE. The gold I gave to Dromio is laid up
    Safe at the Centaur; and the heedful slave
    Is wander'd forth, in care to seek me out
    By computation and mine host's report.
    I could not speak with Dromio since at first
    I sent him from the mart. See, here he comes.—

[*Enter* DROMIO *of Syracuse.*]

    How now sir! is your merry humour alter'd?
    As you love strokes, so jest with me again.
    You know no Centaur? you received no gold?
    Your mistress sent to have me home to dinner?
    My house was at the Phoenix? Wast thou mad,
    That thus so madly thou didst answer me?

---

game till lie got near enough to make sure of it. Hence it came to signify *pretence, mask,* or *cover.* And so here, Adriana probably means that she serves but as a cover for her husband, behind or beneath which he hunts such game as he prefers.

    [46] *Dispense* seems to be used rather oddly, not to say loosely, here,—in the sense of *put up with;* which, however, comes pretty near one of its old meanings,—*atone for* or *compensate.*

    [47] *Lets,* here, is the old word, now obsolete, meaning *hinders.*

    [48] *Alone* repeated in slightly-different senses for the sake of a certain jingle, apparently. So in the Poet's *Lucrece:* "But I *alone alone* must sit and pine."

DROMIO OF SYRACUSE. What answer, sir? when spake I such a
    word?
ANTIPHOLUS OF SYRACUSE. Even now, even here, not half an
    hour since.
DROMIO OF SYRACUSE. I did not see you since you sent me hence,
    Home to the Centaur, with the gold you gave me.
ANTIPHOLUS OF SYRACUSE. Villain, thou didst deny the gold's
    receipt,
    And told'st me of a mistress and a dinner;
    For which, I hope, thou felt'st I was displeased.
DROMIO OF SYRACUSE. I am glad to see you in this merry vein:
    What means this jest? I pray you, master, tell me.
ANTIPHOLUS OF SYRACUSE. Yea, dost thou jeer and flout me in
    the teeth?
    Think'st thou I jest? Hold, take thou that, and that.

[Beating him.]

DROMIO OF SYRACUSE. Hold, sir, for God's sake! now your jest is
    earnest:
    Upon what bargain do you give it me?
ANTIPHOLUS OF SYRACUSE. Because that I familiarly sometimes
    Do use you for my fool and chat with you,
    Your sauciness will jest upon[49] my love
    And make a common[50] of my serious hours.
    When the sun shines let foolish gnats make sport,
    But creep in crannies when he hides his beams.
    If you will jest with me, know my aspect,
    And fashion your demeanor to my looks,
    Or I will beat this method in your sconce.
DROMIO OF SYRACUSE. Sconce call you it? so you would leave
    battering, I had rather have it a head: an you use these blows long,
    I must get a sconce for my head and ensconce it too; or else I shall
    seek my wit in my shoulders. But, I pray, sir why am I beaten?
ANTIPHOLUS OF SYRACUSE. Dost thou not know?
DROMIO OF SYRACUSE. Nothing, sir, but that I am beaten.
ANTIPHOLUS OF SYRACUSE. Shall I tell you why?
DROMIO OF SYRACUSE. Ay, sir, and wherefore; for they say every
    why hath a wherefore.

---

    [49] The Poet several times has *jet upon* in the sense of *encroach upon.* So in *King
Richard III.,* ii. 4: "Insulting tyranny begins to *jet upon* the innocent and aweless throne."
Also in the play of *Sir Thomas More,* quoted by Dyce: "It is hard when Englishmens
paciunce must be thus *jetted on* by straungers."
    [50] *Common* is land unenclosed, and so made free with or used in common by the
people, whether for pleasure, play, or pasturage.

ANTIPHOLUS OF SYRACUSE. Why, first, for flouting me; and then, wherefore,—

For urging it the second time to me.

DROMIO OF SYRACUSE. Was there ever any man thus beaten out of season,

When in the why and the wherefore is neither rhyme nor reason? Well, sir, I thank you.

ANTIPHOLUS OF SYRACUSE. Thank me, sir, for what?

DROMIO OF SYRACUSE. Marry, sir, for this something that you gave me for nothing.

ANTIPHOLUS OF SYRACUSE. I'll make you amends next, to give you nothing for something. But say, sir, is it dinner-time?

DROMIO OF SYRACUSE. No, sir; I think the meat wants that I have.

ANTIPHOLUS OF SYRACUSE. In good time, sir; what's that?

DROMIO OF SYRACUSE. Basting.

ANTIPHOLUS OF SYRACUSE. Well, sir, then 'twill be dry.

DROMIO OF SYRACUSE. If it be, sir, I pray you, eat none of it.

ANTIPHOLUS OF SYRACUSE. Your reason?

DROMIO OF SYRACUSE. Lest it make you choleric,[51] and purchase me another dry basting.

ANTIPHOLUS OF SYRACUSE. Well, sir, learn to jest in good time: there's a time for all things.

DROMIO OF SYRACUSE. I durst have denied that, before you were so choleric.

ANTIPHOLUS OF SYRACUSE. By what rule, sir?

DROMIO OF SYRACUSE. Marry, sir, by a rule as plain as the plain bald pate of father Time himself.

ANTIPHOLUS OF SYRACUSE. Let's hear it.

DROMIO OF SYRACUSE. There's no time for a man to recover his hair that grows bald by nature.

ANTIPHOLUS OF SYRACUSE. May he not do it by fine and recovery?[52]

DROMIO OF SYRACUSE. Yes, to pay a fine for a periwig and recover the lost hair of another man.

ANTIPHOLUS OF SYRACUSE. Why is Time such a niggard of hair, being, as it is, so plentiful an excrement?[53]

DROMIO OF SYRACUSE. Because it is a blessing that he bestows on

---

[51] Such was thought to be the effect of meats so much done as to be undone. In the *Taming of the Shrew*, iv. 1, Petruchio sends off the meat because "'twas burnt and dried away; and I expressly am forbid to touch it, for it *engenders choler*."

[52] *Fine and recovery* is the name of an old legal process, now out of use, for testing and assuring the tenure of property. Ritson, a lawyer, describes it as "the strongest assurance known to English law."

[53] *Excrement* from *excrescere, to grow forth*, was used of whatever seems to vegetate from the body, such as hair, beard, and nails.

beasts; and what he hath scanted men in hair he hath given them in wit.

ANTIPHOLUS OF SYRACUSE. Why, but there's many a man hath more hair than wit.[54]

DROMIO OF SYRACUSE. Not a man of those but he hath the wit to lose his hair.[55]

ANTIPHOLUS OF SYRACUSE. Why, thou didst conclude hairy men plain dealers without wit.

DROMIO OF SYRACUSE. The plainer dealer, the sooner lost: yet he loseth it in a kind of jollity.

ANTIPHOLUS OF SYRACUSE. For what reason?

DROMIO OF SYRACUSE. For two; and sound ones too.

ANTIPHOLUS OF SYRACUSE. Nay, not sound, I pray you.

DROMIO OF SYRACUSE. Sure ones, then.

ANTIPHOLUS OF SYRACUSE. Nay, not sure, in a thing falsing.

DROMIO OF SYRACUSE. Certain ones then.

ANTIPHOLUS OF SYRACUSE. Name them.

DROMIO OF SYRACUSE. The one, to save the money that he spends in trimming; the other, that at dinner they should not drop in his porridge.

ANTIPHOLUS OF SYRACUSE. You would all this time have proved there is no time for all things.

DROMIO OF SYRACUSE. Marry, and did, sir; namely, no time to recover hair lost by nature.

ANTIPHOLUS OF SYRACUSE. But your reason was not substantial, why there is no time to recover.

DROMIO OF SYRACUSE. Thus I mend it: Time himself is bald and therefore to the world's end will have bald followers.

ANTIPHOLUS OF SYRACUSE. I knew 'twould be a bald conclusion: But, soft! who wafts[56] us yonder?

[*Enter* ADRIANA *and* LUCIANA.]

ADRIANA. Ay, ay, Antipholus, look strange and frown:
Some other mistress hath thy sweet aspects;
I am not Adriana nor thy wife.

---

[54] This expression seems to have been proverbial. It is well illustrated in the following lines, 1656, upon Suckling's *Aglaura*, which was printed in folio:

This great voluminous pamphlet may be said
To be like one that hath more hair than head;
More excrement than body:—trees which sprout
With broadest leaves have still the smallest fruit.

[55] Alluding to the loss of hair by what was called the French disease.
[56] To *waft* is to *beckon with the hand.*

The time was once when thou unurged wouldst vow
That never words were music to thine ear,
That never object pleasing in thine eye,
That never touch well welcome to thy hand,
That never meat sweet-savor'd in thy taste,
Unless I spake, or look'd, or touch'd, or carved to thee.
How comes it now, my husband, O, how comes it,
That thou art thus estranged from thyself?
Thyself I call it, being strange to me,
That, undividable, incorporate,
Am better than thy dear self's better part.
Ah, do not tear away thyself from me!
For know, my love, as easy mayest thou fall[57]
A drop of water in the breaking gulf,
And take unmingled that same drop again,
Without addition or diminishing,
As take from me thyself and not me too.
How dearly would it touch me to the quick,
Shouldst thou but hear I were licentious
And that this body, consecrate to thee,
By ruffian lust should be contaminate!
Wouldst thou not spit at me and spurn at me
And hurl the name of husband in my face
And tear the stain'd skin off my harlot-brow
And from my false hand cut the wedding-ring
And break it with a deep-divorcing vow?
I know thou canst; and therefore see thou do it.
I am possess'd with an adulterate blot;
My blood is mingled with the crime of lust:
For if we too be one and thou play false,
I do digest the poison of thy flesh,
Being strumpeted by thy contagion.
Keep then far league and truce with thy true bed;
I live unstain'd, thou undishonoured.

ANTIPHOLUS OF SYRACUSE. Plead you to me, fair dame? I know
    you not:
In Ephesus I am but two hours old,
As strange unto your town as to your talk;
Who, every word by all my wit being scann'd,
Want wit in all one word to understand.

LUCIANA. Fie, brother! how the world is changed with you!
When were you wont to use my sister thus?
She sent for you by Dromio home to dinner.

---

[57] *Fall* as a transitive verb; *let fall.* Often so.

ANTIPHOLUS OF SYRACUSE. By Dromio?

DROMIO OF SYRACUSE. By me?

ADRIANA. By thee; and this thou didst return from him,
That he did buffet thee, and, in his blows,
Denied my house for his, me for his wife.

ANTIPHOLUS OF SYRACUSE. Did you converse, sir, with this
gentlewoman?
What is the course and drift of your compact?

DROMIO OF SYRACUSE. I, sir? I never saw her till this time.

ANTIPHOLUS OF SYRACUSE. Villain, thou liest; for even her very
words
Didst thou deliver to me on the mart.

DROMIO OF SYRACUSE. I never spake with her in all my life.

ANTIPHOLUS OF SYRACUSE. How can she thus then call us by our
names,
Unless it be by inspiration.

ADRIANA. How ill agrees it with your gravity
To counterfeit thus grossly with your slave,
Abetting him to thwart me in my mood!
Be it my wrong you are from me exempt,[58]
But wrong not that wrong with a more contempt.
Come, I will fasten on this sleeve of thine:
Thou art an elm, my husband,—I a vine,[59]
Whose weakness, married to thy stronger state,
Makes me with thy strength to communicate:
If aught possess thee from me, it is dross,
Usurping ivy, brier, or idle[60] moss;
Who, all for want of pruning, with intrusion
Infect thy sap and live on thy confusion.

ANTIPHOLUS OF SYRACUSE. [*Aside.*] To me she speaks; she
moves me for her theme:
What, was I married to her in my dream?
Or sleep I now and think I hear all this?
What error drives our eyes and ears amiss?
Until I know this sure uncertainty,
I'll entertain the offer'd fallacy.

LUCIANA. Dromio, go bid the servants spread for dinner.

---

[58] An odd use of *exempt*, meaning *farted, separated,* or *taken away.* So in a letter from the Earl of Nottingham in favour of Edward Alleyn, cited by Malone: "Situate in a very remote and *exempt* place near Goulding Lane."

[59] So in *Paradise Lost,* v. 215: "Or they led the vine to wed her elm: she, spoused, about him twines her marriageable arms." Douce remarks that there is something extremely beautiful in making the vine the lawful spouse of the elm, and the *parasite* plants here named its *concubines.*

[60] *Idle* is *unfruitful* or *useless;* as in *Othello,* i. 3: "Of antres vast and deserts *idle.*"

DROMIO OF SYRACUSE. O, for my beads! I cross me for a sinner.
    This is the fairy land;—O spite of spites!—
    We talk with goblins, owls and sprites:
    If we obey them not, this will ensue,—
    They'll suck our breath, or pinch us black and blue.
LUCIANA. Why pratest thou to thyself and answer'st not?
    Dromio, thou drone, thou snail, thou slug, thou sot!
DROMIO OF SYRACUSE. I am transformed, master, am I not?
ANTIPHOLUS OF SYRACUSE. I think thou art in mind, and so am I.
DROMIO OF SYRACUSE. Nay, master, both in mind and in my
    shape.
ANTIPHOLUS OF SYRACUSE. Thou hast thine own form.
DROMIO OF SYRACUSE. No, I am an ape.
LUCIANA. If thou art changed to aught, 'tis to an ass.
DROMIO OF SYRACUSE. 'Tis true; she rides me and I long for grass.
    'Tis so, I am an ass; else it could never be
    But I should know her as well as she knows me.
ADRIANA. Come, come, no longer will I be a fool,
    To put the finger in the eye and weep,
    Whilst man and master laugh my woes to scorn.—
    Come, sir, to dinner.—Dromio, keep the gate.—
    Husband, I'll dine above with you to-day
    And shrive you[61] of a thousand idle pranks.—
    Sirrah, if any ask you for your master,
    Say he dines forth, and let no creature enter.—
    Come, sister.—Dromio, play the porter well.
ANTIPHOLUS OF SYRACUSE. [*Aside.*] Am I in earth, in Heaven, or
    in Hell?
    Sleeping or waking? mad or well-advised?
    Known unto these, and to myself disguised!
    I'll say as they say and persever so,
    And in this mist at all adventures go.
DROMIO OF SYRACUSE. Master, shall I be porter at the gate?
ADRIANA. Ay; and let none enter, lest I break your pate.
LUCIANA. Come, come, Antipholus, we dine too late. [*Exeunt.*]

---

[61] "*Shrive* you" is *confess* you, or call on you to confess. To *impose penance* is one part of a confessor's office.

ACT III.

SCENE I.

Before the house of ANTIPHOLUS *of Ephesus.*

[*Enter* ANTIPHOLUS *of Ephesus,* DROMIO *of Ephesus,* ANGELO, *and* BALTHAZAR.]

ANTIPHOLUS OF EPHESUS. Good Signior Angelo, you must excuse
    us all;
  My wife is shrewish when I keep not hours:
  Say that I linger'd with you at your shop
  To see the making of her carcanet,[62]
  And that to-morrow you will bring it home.
  But here's a villain that would face me down
  He met me on the mart, and that I beat him,[63]
  And charged him with a thousand marks in gold,
  And that I did deny my wife and house.—
  Thou drunkard, thou, what didst thou mean by this?
DROMIO OF EPHESUS. Say what you will, sir, but I know what I
    know;
  That you beat me at the mart, I have your hand to show:
  If the skin were parchment, and the blows you gave were ink,
  Your own handwriting would tell you what I think.
ANTIPHOLUS OF EPHESUS. I think thou art an ass.
DROMIO OF EPHESUS. Marry,[64] so it doth appear
  By the wrongs I suffer and the blows I bear.
  I should kick, being kick'd; and, being at that pass,
  You would keep from my heels and beware of an ass.
ANTIPHOLUS OF EPHESUS. You're sad, Signior Balthazar: pray
    God our cheer
  May answer my good will and your good welcome here.
BALTHAZAR. I hold your dainties cheap, sir, and your welcome dear.
ANTIPHOLUS OF EPHESUS. O, Signior Balthazar, either at flesh or
    fish,
  A table full of welcome make scarce one dainty dish.

---

[62] A *carcanet* is a *necklace;* later in the play it is called a *chain.*

[63] "Would *convince* me *that* he met me on the mart, and that I beat him," is the
meaning.

[64] *Marry* was much used as a general intensive, meaning *indeed, verily, to be sure.*
It grew into use from a custom of swearing or affirming by the Virgin Mary; much the
same as *heracle* and *edepol* in Latin; the latter being originally an oath by Castor and
Pollux.

BALTHAZAR. Good meat, sir, is common; that every churl affords.

ANTIPHOLUS OF EPHESUS. And welcome more common; for that's
    nothing but words.

BALTHAZAR. Small cheer and great welcome makes a merry feast.

ANTIPHOLUS OF EPHESUS. Ay, to a niggardly host, and more
    sparing guest:

    But though my cates[65] be mean, take them in good part;

    Better cheer may you have, but not with better heart.

    But, soft![66] my door is lock'd.—Go bid them let us in.

DROMIO OF EPHESUS. Maud, Bridget, Marian, Cicely, Gillian,
    Ginn!

DROMIO OF SYRACUSE. [*Within.*] Mome, malt-horse, capon,
    coxcomb, idiot, patch![67]

    Either get thee from the door, or sit down at the hatch.

    Dost thou conjure for wenches, that thou call'st for such store,

    When one is one too many? Go, get thee from the door.

DROMIO OF EPHESUS. What patch is made our porter? My master
    stays in the street.

DROMIO OF SYRACUSE. [*Within.*] Let him walk from whence he
    came, lest he catch cold on's feet.

ANTIPHOLUS OF EPHESUS. Who talks within there? ho, open the
    door!

DROMIO OF SYRACUSE. [*Within.*] Right, sir; I'll tell you when, an
    you tell me wherefore.

ANTIPHOLUS OF EPHESUS. Wherefore? for my dinner: I have not
    dined to-day.

DROMIO OF SYRACUSE. [*Within.*] Nor to-day here you must not;
    come again when you may.

ANTIPHOLUS OF EPHESUS. What art thou that keepest me out from
    the house I owe?[68]

DROMIO OF SYRACUSE. [*Within.*] The porter for this time, sir, and
    my name is Dromio.

DROMIO OF EPHESUS. O villain! thou hast stolen both mine office
    and my name.

    The one ne'er got me credit, the other mickle blame.

---

[65] *Cates* is an old form for *cakes*, but sometimes used, as here, in the wider sense of
viands or *food*, especially of *dainties*.

[66] *Soft!* was a common exclamative meaning about the same as *stay, hold,* or *not too
fast.*

[67] All these are old terms of abuse, forming a part of that extensive vocabulary
called Billingsgate, which was the name of a place in London where loud and coarse
women sold fish. *Mome,* of uncertain origin, comes pretty near *blockhead. Malt-horse* is
a *brewer's horse,* a dull, dumpish beast. *Capon* is a rooster emasculated, and fatted for
the table. *Patch,* applied to the "allowed Fool," on account of motley or *patchwork* dress,
came to be used of a natural fool.

[68] *Owe,* a shortened form of *owen,* is *own* or *possess.*

If thou hadst been Dromio to-day in my place,

Thou wouldst have changed thy face for a name or thy name for an ass.

LUCE. [*Within.*] What a coil[69] is there, Dromio? who are those at the gate?

DROMIO OF EPHESUS. Let my master in, Luce.

LUCE. [*Within.*] Faith, no; he comes too late;

And so tell your master.

DROMIO OF EPHESUS. O Lord, I must laugh!

Have at you with a proverb—*Shall I set in my staff?*

LUCE. [*Within.*] Have at you with another; that's, *When? can you tell?*

DROMIO OF SYRACUSE. If thy name be call'd Lucs—Luce, thou hast answered him well.[70]

ANTIPHOLUS OF EPHESUS. Do you hear, you minion? you'll let us in, I hope?

LUCE. [*Within.*] I thought to have asked you.

DROMIO OF SYRACUSE. [*Within.*] And you said no.

DROMIO OF EPHESUS. So, come, help: well struck! there was blow for blow.

ANTIPHOLUS OF EPHESUS. Thou baggage, let me in.

LUCE. [*Within.*] Can you tell for whose sake?

DROMIO OF EPHESUS.

Master, knock the door hard.

LUCE. [*Within.*] Let him knock till it ache.

ANTIPHOLUS OF EPHESUS. You'll cry for this, minion, if I beat the door down.

LUCE. [*Within.*] What needs all that, and a pair of stocks[71] in the town?

ADRIANA. [*Within.*] Who is that at the door that keeps all this noise?

DROMIO OF SYRACUSE. [*Within.*] By my troth, your town is troubled with unruly boys.

ANTIPHOLUS OF EPHESUS. Are you there, wife? you might have come before.

ADRIANA. [*Within.*] Your wife, sir knave! go get you from the door.

DROMIO OF EPHESUS. If you went in pain, master, this knave would go sore.

ANGELO. Here is neither cheer, sir, nor welcome: we would fain have either.

BALTHAZAR. In debating which was best, we shall part[72] with

---

[69] *Coil* is *hubbub, rumpus, fuss;* often so used in the Poet's time.

[70] *Luce* is an old name for the fish called *pike;* which seems to be the turning-point of the quibble here. Perhaps the sense of *thrusting with a pike* is implied, as Luce has aptly met proverb with proverb.

[71] "A pair of stocks" was a machine in which certain offenders were fastened by the ankles, for punishment; the offender being forced to sit with his legs in a horizontal position.

neither.

DROMIO OF EPHESUS. They stand at the door, master; bid them
 welcome hither.

ANTIPHOLUS OF EPHESUS. There is something in the wind, that we
 cannot get in.

DROMIO OF EPHESUS. You would say so, master, if your garments
 were thin.

 Your cake there is warm within; you stand here in the cold:

 It would make a man mad as a buck, to be so bought and sold.[73]

ANTIPHOLUS OF EPHESUS. Go fetch me something: I'll break ope
 the gate.

DROMIO OF SYRACUSE. [*Within.*] Break any breaking here, and I'll
 break your knave's pate.

DROMIO OF EPHESUS. A man may break a word with you, sir, and
 words are but wind,

 Ay, and break it in your face, so he break it not behind.

DROMIO OF SYRACUSE. [*Within.*] It seems thou want'st breaking:
 out upon thee, hind!

DROMIO OF EPHESUS. Here's too much *out upon thee*! I pray thee,
 let me in.

DROMIO OF SYRACUSE. [*Within.*] Ay, when fowls have no feathers
 and fish have no fin.

ANTIPHOLUS OF EPHESUS. Well, I'll break in: go borrow me a
 crow.

DROMIO OF EPHESUS. A crow without feather? Master, mean you
 so?

 For a fish without a fin, there's a fowl without a feather:

 If a crow help us in, sirrah, we'll pluck a crow together.[74]

ANTIPHOLUS OF EPHESUS. Go get thee gone; fetch me an iron
 crow.

BALTHAZAR. Have patience, sir; O, let it not be so!

 Herein you war against your reputation

 And draw within the compass of suspect[75]

 The unviolated honour of your wife.

 Once this,[76]—your long experience of her wisdom,

 Her sober virtue, years and modesty,

 Plead on her part some cause to you unknown:

---

  [72] *Part* for *depart;* the two being formerly used indiscriminately.

  [73] This phrase, now so common, for *tricked, taken in,* or *hoaxed,* is here seen to be
as old as Shakespeare's time, at least.

  [74] This Dromio seems to be in a flux of proverbs. To "pluck a crow together" was a
proverbial phrase for *having a quarrel* or *a fight.*

  [75] Another instance like that of *dispose.* See page 10, note 4.

  [76] *Once this* is plainly equivalent, here, to *this is enough.* So in *Much Ado,* i. 1:
"Look, what will serve, is fit: '*tis once* thou lovest; and I will fit thee with the remedy."
And in *Coriolanus,* ii, 3: "*Once,* if he do require our voices; we ought not to deny him."

And doubt not, sir, but she will well excuse
Why at this time the doors are made[77] against you.
Be ruled by me: depart in patience,
And let us to the Tiger[78] all to dinner,
And about evening come yourself alone
To know the reason of this strange restraint.
If by strong hand you offer to break in
Now in the stirring passage of the day,
A vulgar comment will be made of it,
And that supposed by the common rout
Against your yet ungalled estimation
That may with foul intrusion enter in
And dwell upon your grave when you are dead;
For slander lives upon succession,
For ever housed where it gets possession.
ANTIPHOLUS OF EPHESUS. You have prevailed: I will depart in
    quiet,
And, in despite of mirth,[79] mean to be merry.
I know a wench of excellent discourse,
Pretty and witty; wild, and yet, too, gentle:
There will we dine. This woman that I mean,
My wife—but, I protest, without desert—
Hath oftentimes upbraided me withal:
To her will we to dinner.—Get you home
And fetch the chain; by this I know 'tis made:
Bring it, I pray you, to the Porpentine;[80]
For there's the house: that chain will I bestow—
Be it for nothing but to spite my wife—
Upon mine hostess there: good sir, make haste.
Since mine own doors refuse to entertain me,
I'll knock elsewhere, to see if they'll disdain me.
ANGELO. I'll meet you at that place some hour hence.
ANTIPHOLUS OF EPHESUS. Do so. This jest shall cost me some
    expense. [*Exeunt.*]

[*Enter, from the House,* LUCIANA *and* ANTIPHOLUS *of
    Syracuse.*]

---

[77] To "*make* the doors" is to *fasten* them. Still so used sometimes.

[78] *Tiger*, like *Centaur* and *Phœnix* before, for the name of an inn.

[79] One might think this ought to be "in despite of *grief.*" But he probably means that, to *spite* the mirth his wife is having with another man, he will go and be merry with another woman. Heath explains it thus: "Though mirth hath withdrawn herself from me, and seems determined to avoid me, yet, in despite of her, and whether she will or not, I am resolved to be merry."

[80] *Porpentine* is the old form, always used by Shakespeare, for *porcupine.* Here it is the name of an inn.—*By this*, in the line before, is *by this time.*

LUCIANA. And may it be that you have quite forgot
    A husband's office? shall, Antipholus.
    Even in the spring of love, thy love-springs[81] rot?
    Shall love, in building, grow so ruinous?
    If you did wed my sister for her wealth,
    Then for her wealth's sake use her with more kindness:
    Or if you like elsewhere, do it by stealth;
    Muffle your false love with some show of blindness:
    Let not my sister read it in your eye;
    Be not thy tongue thy own shame's orator;
    Look sweet, be fair, become disloyalty;[82]
    Apparel vice like virtue's harbinger;
    Bear a fair presence, though your heart be tainted;
    Teach sin the carriage of a holy saint;
    Be secret-false: what need she be acquainted?
    What simple thief brags of his own attaint?
    'Tis double wrong, to truant with your bed
    And let her read it in thy looks at board:
    Shame hath a bastard fame, well managed;
    Ill deeds are doubled with an evil word.
    Alas, poor women! make us but believe,
    Being compact of credit,[83] that you love us;
    Though others have the arm, show us the sleeve;
    We in your motion turn and you may move us.
    Then, gentle brother, get you in again;
    Comfort my sister, cheer her, call her wife:
    'Tis holy sport to be a little vain,[84]
    When the sweet breath of flattery conquers strife.
ANTIPHOLUS OF SYRACUSE. Sweet mistress,—what your name is
    else, I know not,
    Nor by what wonder you do hit of[85] mine,—
    Less in your knowledge and your grace you show not
    Than our earth's wonder, more than earth divine.
    Teach me, dear creature, how to think and speak;
    Lay open to my earthy-gross conceit,
    Smother'd in errors, feeble, shallow, weak,

---

[81] *Love-springs* are the *buds of love*, or rather the young *shoots*. So in *Venus and Adonis:* "This canker that eats up love's tender *spring*." And in Baret's *Alvearie:* "The spring, or young *shoots* that grow out of the stems or roots of trees."

[82] To "*become* disloyalty" is to *make it look becoming.*

[83] "*Compact* of *credit*" is *composed, framed,* or *made up* of *credulity.* So in *A Midsummer*, v. i: "The lunatic, the lover, and the poet are of imagination all *compact!*"

[84] *Vain* here means *light of tongue;* speaking falsely or insincerely, as in "the sweet breath of flattery."

[85] *Of* and *on* were used indifferently in such cases. Shakespeare has many instances.

The folded meaning of your words' deceit.
Against my soul's pure truth why labour you
To make it wander in an unknown field?
Are you a god? would you create me new?
Transform me then, and to your power I'll yield.
But if that I am I, then well I know
Your weeping sister is no wife of mine,
Nor to her bed no homage do I owe
Far more, far more to you do I decline.[86]
O, train me not, sweet mermaid, with thy note,
To drown me in thy sister's flood of tears:
Sing, siren, for thyself and I will dote:
Spread o'er the silver waves thy golden hairs,
And as a bed I'll take them and there lie,
And in that glorious supposition think
He gains by death that hath such means to die:
Let Love, being light, be drowned if she sink![87]

LUCIANA. What, are you mad, that you do reason so?

ANTIPHOLUS OF SYRACUSE. Not mad, but mated;[88] how, I do not
know.

LUCIANA. It is a fault that springeth from your eye.

ANTIPHOLUS OF SYRACUSE. For gazing on your beams, fair sun,
being by.

LUCIANA. Gaze where you should, and that will clear your sight.

ANTIPHOLUS OF SYRACUSE. As good to wink, sweet love, as look
on night.

LUCIANA. Why call you me love? call my sister so.

ANTIPHOLUS OF SYRACUSE. Thy sister's sister.

LUCIANA. That's my sister.

ANTIPHOLUS OF SYRACUSE. No;
It is thyself, mine own self's better part,
Mine eye's clear eye, my dear heart's dearer heart,
My food, my fortune and my sweet hope's aim,
My sole earth's Heaven and my Heaven's claim.[89]

---

[86] It appears that *decline* was sometimes used in the sense of *incline*. So Baret: "To
decline; to turne, or hang *toward* some place or thing."

[87] *Love* here means the Queen of love, Venus, not her tow-head son. So in the
Poet's *Venus and Adonis:*

Love is a spirit, all compact of fire,
Not gross to *sink,* but *light,* and will aspire.

[88] A quibble, *mated* being used in the two senses of *matched* and *confounded* or
bewildered. Shakespeare has it repeatedly in the latter sense.

[89] Meaning, probably, "all the happiness I wish for on Earth, and all that I claim
from Heaven hereafter."

LUCIANA. All this my sister is, or else should be.

ANTIPHOLUS OF SYRACUSE. Call thyself sister, sweet, for I am thee.[90]

    Thee will I love and with thee lead my life:

    Thou hast no husband yet nor I no wife.

    Give me thy hand.

LUCIANA. O, soft, air! hold you still:

    I'll fetch my sister, to get her good will. [*Exit.*]

[*Enter, from the House,* DROMIO *of Syracuse running.*]

ANTIPHOLUS OF SYRACUSE. Why, how now, Dromio! where runn'st thou so fast?

DROMIO OF SYRACUSE. Do you know me, sir? am I Dromio? am I your man? am I myself.[91]

ANTIPHOLUS OF SYRACUSE. Thou art Dromio, thou art my man, thou art thyself.

DROMIO OF SYRACUSE. I am an ass, I am a woman's man and besides myself.

ANTIPHOLUS. What woman's man? and how besides thyself? besides thyself?

DROMIO OF SYRACUSE. Marry, sir, besides myself, I am due to a woman; one that claims me, one that haunts me, one that will have me.

ANTIPHOLUS OF SYRACUSE. What claim lays she to thee?

DROMIO OF SYRACUSE. Marry sir, such claim as you would lay to your horse; and she would have me as a beast: not that, I being a beast, she would have me; but that she, being a very beastly creature, lays claim to me.

ANTIPHOLUS OF SYRACUSE. What is she?

DROMIO OF SYRACUSE. A very reverent body; ay, such a one as a man may not speak of without he say *sir-reverence.*[92] I have but lean luck in the match, and yet is she a wondrous fat marriage.

ANTIPHOLUS OF SYRACUSE. How dost thou mean,—a fat marriage?

DROMIO OF SYRACUSE. Marry, sir, she's the kitchen wench and all grease; and I know not what use to put her to but to make a lamp of

---

[90] *Aim thee* sounds harsh, but evidently means *aim at thee;* that is, *seek* thee. So in *Paradise Regained,* iv. 208: "Me nought advantaged, missing *what I aim'd.*"

[91] The two forms *beside* and *besides* had not become differentiated into preposition and adverb in Shakespeare's time. Here it is necessary to retain the adverbial form in the prepositional sense, on account of the quibble in the second speech below.

[92] *Sir-reverence* is an old corruption of *salva reverentia* or *save reverence*, a shortened form of "saving your reverence," which was much used as an apologetic phrase for introducing any coarse or profane expression or allusion.

her and run from her by her own light. I warrant, her rags and the tallow in them will burn a Poland winter: if she lives till doomsday, she'll burn a week longer than the whole world.

ANTIPHOLUS OF SYRACUSE. What complexion is she of?

DROMIO OF SYRACUSE. Swart,[93] like my shoe, but her face nothing half so clean kept: for why[94] she sweats; a man may go over shoes in the grime of it.

ANTIPHOLUS OF SYRACUSE. That's a fault that water will mend.

DROMIO OF SYRACUSE. No, sir, 'tis in grain; Noah's flood could not do it.

ANTIPHOLUS OF SYRACUSE. What's her name?

DROMIO OF SYRACUSE. Nell, sir; but her name and three quarters, that's an ell and three quarters, will not measure her from hip to hip.

ANTIPHOLUS OF SYRACUSE. Then she bears some breadth?

DROMIO OF SYRACUSE. No longer from head to foot than from hip to hip: she is spherical, like a globe; I could find out countries in her.

ANTIPHOLUS OF SYRACUSE. In what part of her body stands Ireland?

DROMIO OF SYRACUSE. Marry, in her buttocks: I found it out by the bogs.

ANTIPHOLUS OF SYRACUSE. Where Scotland?

DROMIO OF SYRACUSE. I found it by the barrenness; hard in the palm of the hand.

ANTIPHOLUS OF SYRACUSE. Where France?

DROMIO OF SYRACUSE. In her forehead; armed and reverted, making war against her hair.[95]

ANTIPHOLUS OF SYRACUSE. Where England?

DROMIO OF SYRACUSE. I looked for the chalky cliffs, but I could find no whiteness in them; but I guess it stood in her chin, by the salt rheum that ran between France and it.

ANTIPHOLUS OF SYRACUSE. Where Spain?

---

[93] *Swart* or *swarth* is *dark, dusky,* or *swarthy.*

[94] *For why* is here a simple equivalent of *because,* or *for the reason that.* The usage was ancient and common, and was fast passing away in the Poet's time; but he has several instances of it. So in *The Two Gentlemen,* iii. 1: "If she do chide, 'tis not to have you gone; *for why* the fools are mad, if left alone." And in the fine old ballad, *My Mind to me a Kingdom Is:* "To none of these I yield as thrall, *for why* my mind despiseth all." Also in *A Warning for Faire Women,* 1599: "What time a day is't now? it cannot be imagin'd by the *sunne, for why* I have not scene it shine to daie."

[95] A quibble, of course, between *hair* and *heir;* alluding to the War of the League against Henry of Navarre, who became heir to the crown of France in 1589.—The sense and application of *reverted* are here very obscure, to say the least. The word itself means *turned* or *thrown back.* The arming is, I take it, with the French disease, which made war against the hair in causing baldness. The jest about the disease in question is repeated, *ad nauseam,* in old plays.

DROMIO OF SYRACUSE. Faith, I saw it not; but I felt it hot in her breath.

ANTIPHOLUS OF SYRACUSE. Where America, the Indies?

DROMIO OF SYRACUSE. Oh, sir, upon her nose all o'er embellished with rubies, carbuncles, sapphires, declining their rich aspect to the hot breath of Spain; who sent whole armadas of carracks to be ballast[96] at her nose.

ANTIPHOLUS OF SYRACUSE. Where stood Belgia, the Netherlands?

DROMIO OF SYRACUSE. Oh, sir, I did not look so low. To conclude, this drudge, or diviner, laid claim to me, call'd me Dromio; swore I was assured to her; told me what privy marks I had about me, as, the mark of my shoulder, the mole in my neck, the great wart on my left arm, that I amazed ran from her as a witch:

> And, I think, if my breast had not been made of faith and my heart of steel,
> She had transform'd me to a curtal dog and made me turn i' the wheel.[97]

ANTIPHOLUS OF SYRACUSE. Go hie thee presently, post to the road:
An if the wind blow any way from shore,
I will not harbour in this town to-night:
If any bark put forth, come to the mart,
Where I will walk till thou return to me.
If every one knows us and we know none,
'Tis time, I think, to trudge, pack and be gone.

DROMIO OF SYRACUSE. As from a bear a man would run for life,
So fly I from her that would be my wife. [*Exit.*]

ANTIPHOLUS OF SYRACUSE. There's none but witches do inhabit here;
And therefore 'tis high time that I were hence.
She that doth call me husband, even my soul
Doth for a wife abhor. But her fair sister,
Possess'd with such a gentle sovereign grace,
Of such enchanting presence and discourse,
Hath almost made me traitor to myself:
But, lest myself be guilty to[98] self-wrong,

---

[96] *Ballast* for *ballasted*, or furnished with ballast.—A *carack* was a large ship of burden; from the Spanish *caraca*.

[97] Dogs were sometimes used for working the wheels of turnspits, when meats were roasted before the fire. See page 16, note 26.

[98] *Guilty to* a thing sounds odd; but the Poet has it again in *The Winter's Tale*, iv. 3: "Th' unthought-on accident is *guilty to* what we wildly do."

I'll stop mine ears against the mermaid's song.

[*Re-enter* ANGELO *with the Chain.*]

ANGELO. Master Antipholus,—
ANTIPHOLUS OF SYRACUSE. Ay, that's my name.
ANGELO. I know it well, sir, lo, here is the chain.
    I thought to have ta'en you at the Porpentine:
    The chain unfinish'd made me stay thus long.
ANTIPHOLUS OF SYRACUSE. [*Taking the chain.*] What is your will
        that I shall do with this?
ANGELO. What please yourself, sir: I have made it for you.
ANTIPHOLUS OF SYRACUSE. Made it for me, sir! I bespoke it not.
ANGELO. Not once, nor twice, but twenty times you have.
    Go home with it and please your wife withal;
    And soon at supper-time I'll visit you
    And then receive my money for the chain.
ANTIPHOLUS OF SYRACUSE. I pray you, sir, receive the money
      now,
    For fear you ne'er see chain nor money more.
ANGELO. You are a merry man, sir: fare you well. [*Exit.*]
ANTIPHOLUS OF SYRACUSE. What I should think of this, I cannot
      tell:
    But this I think, there's no man is so vain
    That would refuse so fair an offer'd chain.[99]
    I see a man here needs not live by shifts,
    When in the streets he meets such golden gifts.
    I'll to the mart, and there for Dromio stay
    If any ship put out, then straight away. [*Exit.*]

---

[99] That is, "so fair-offer'd a chain," or so fairly offer'd. So in *Love's Labours Lost,*
i. 1: "Having sworn too hard-a-keeping oath."

ACT IV.

SCENE I.

A public Place.

[*Enter Second* MERCHANT, ANGELO, *and an* OFFICER.]

SECOND MERCHANT. You know since Pentecost the sum is due,
 And since I have not much importuned you;
 Nor now I had not, but that I am bound
 To Persia, and want guilders for my voyage:
 Therefore make present satisfaction,
 Or I'll attach you by this officer.
ANGELO. Even just the sum that I do owe to you
 Is growing[100] to me by Antipholus,
 And in the instant that I met with you
 He had of me a chain: at five o'clock
 I shall receive the money for the same.
 Pleaseth you walk with me down to his house,
 I will discharge my bond and thank you too.

[*Enter* ANTIPHOLUS *of Ephesus and* DROMIO *of Ephesus.*]

OFFICER. That labour may you save: see where he comes.
ANTIPHOLUS OF EPHESUS. While I go to the goldsmith's house, go
  thou
 And buy a rope's end: that will I bestow
 Among my wife and her confederates,
 For locking me out of my doors by day.
 But, soft! I see the goldsmith. Get thee gone;
 Buy thou a rope and bring it home to me.
DROMIO OF EPHESUS. I buy a thousand pound a year: I buy a rope.
 [*Exit.*]
ANTIPHOLUS OF EPHESUS. A man is well holp[101] up that trusts to
  you:

---

  [100] *Grow* was sometimes used in the sense of *accrue.*
  [101] *Holp* or *holpen* is the old preterite of *help.*—Of the preceding line, "I buy a thousand pound a-year! I buy a rope!" no satisfactory explanation has been given. Staunton notes, "there may have been an allusion well understood at the time; but which, referring merely to some transitory event, or some popular bye-word of the moment, has passed into oblivion." There is no apparent connection between "buying a thousand pound a-year" and "buying a rope." I can make nothing of it, unless, as the rope is to be used in beating, a poor quibble is intended in *pound;* one of its senses being *poundings.*

I promised your presence and the chain;
But neither chain nor goldsmith came to me.
Belike you thought our love would last too long,
If it were chain'd together, and therefore came not.

ANGELO. Saving your merry humour, here's the note
How much your chain weighs to the utmost carat,
The fineness of the gold and chargeful fashion.
Which doth amount to three odd ducats more
Than I stand debted to this gentleman:
I pray you, see him presently discharged,
For he is bound to sea and stays but for it.

ANTIPHOLUS OF EPHESUS. I am not furnish'd with the present money;
Besides, I have some business in the town.
Good signior, take the stranger to my house
And with you take the chain and bid my wife
Disburse the sum on the receipt thereof:
Perchance I will be there as soon as you.

ANGELO. Then you will bring the chain to her yourself?

ANTIPHOLUS OF EPHESUS. No; bear it with you, lest I come not time enough.

ANGELO. Well, sir, I will. Have you the chain about you?

ANTIPHOLUS OF EPHESUS. An if I have not, sir, I hope you have;
Or else you may return without your money.

ANGELO. Nay, come, I pray you, sir, give me the chain:
Both wind and tide stays for this gentleman,
And I, to blame, have held him here too long.

ANTIPHOLUS OF EPHESUS. Good Lord! you use this dalliance to excuse
Your breach of promise to the Porpentine.
I should have chid you for not bringing it,
But, like a shrew,[102] you first begin to brawl.

SECOND MERCHANT. The hour steals on; I pray you, sir, dispatch.

ANGELO. You hear how he importunes me;—the chain!

ANTIPHOLUS OF EPHESUS. Why, give it to my wife and fetch your money.

ANGELO. Come, come, you know I gave it you even now.
Either send the chain or send me by some token.

ANTIPHOLUS OF EPHESUS. Fie, now you run this humour out of breath, where's the chain? I pray you, let me see it.

SECOND MERCHANT. My business cannot brook this dalliance.
Good sir, say whether you'll answer me or no:
If not, I'll leave him to the officer.

---

[102] In old language, a *shrew* is a *scold;* from *shrewd, sharp-tongued.*

ANTIPHOLUS OF EPHESUS. I answer you! what should I answer
you?

ANGELO. The money that you owe me for the chain.

ANTIPHOLUS OF EPHESUS. I owe you none till I receive the chain.

ANGELO. You know I gave it you half an hour since.

ANTIPHOLUS OF EPHESUS. You gave me none: you wrong me
much to say so.

ANGELO. You wrong me more, sir, in denying it:
Consider how it stands upon my credit.[103]

SECOND MERCHANT. Well, officer, arrest him at my suit.

OFFICER. I do;—
And charge you in the duke's name to obey me.

ANGELO. This touches me in reputation.
Either consent to pay this sum for me
Or I attach you by this officer.—

ANTIPHOLUS OF EPHESUS. Consent to pay thee that I never had!
Arrest me, foolish fellow, if thou darest.

ANGELO. Here is thy fee; arrest him, officer,
I would not spare my brother in this case,
If he should scorn me so apparently.[104]

OFFICER. I do arrest you, sir: you hear the suit.

ANTIPHOLUS OF EPHESUS. I do obey thee till I give thee bail.
But, sirrah, you shall buy this sport as dear
As all the metal in your shop will answer.

ANGELO. Sir, sir, I will have law in Ephesus,
To your notorious shame; I doubt it not.

[*Enter* DROMIO *of Syracuse.*]

DROMIO OF SYRACUSE. Master, there is a bark of Epidamnum
That stays but till her owner comes aboard,
And then, sir, she bears away. Our freightage, sir,
I have convey'd aboard; and I have bought
The oil, the balsamum and aqua-vitae.
The ship is in her trim; the merry wind
Blows fair from land: they stay for nought at all
But for their owner, master, and yourself.

ANTIPHOLUS OF EPHESUS. How now! a madman! Why, thou
peevish[105] sheep,

---

[103] That is, *concerns*, or *is important to*, my credit. The phrase was very common.
So Shelton's translation of *Don Quixote*, 1620: "Tel me your name; for *it stands me very
much upon* to know it."

[104] *Apparently*, here, is *evidently*. The Poet has *apparent* repeatedly in that sense.

[105] *Peevish* is *foolish* or *mad*. Commonly so in Shakespeare.—A quibble is intended
here between *sheep* and *ship*, which appear to have been sounded alike.

What ship of Epidamnum stays for me?

DROMIO OF SYRACUSE. A ship you sent me to, to hire waftage.[106]

ANTIPHOLUS OF EPHESUS. Thou drunken slave, I sent thee for a
    rope;
    And told thee to what purpose and what end.

DROMIO OF SYRACUSE. You sent me for a rope's end as soon:
    You sent me to the bay, sir, for a barque.

ANTIPHOLUS OF EPHESUS. I will debate this matter at more leisure
    And teach your ears to list me with more heed.
    To Adriana, villain, hie thee straight:
    Give her this key, and tell her, in the desk
    That's cover'd o'er with Turkish tapestry,
    There is a purse of ducats; let her send it:
    Tell her I am arrested in the street
    And that shall bail me; hie thee, slave, be gone.—
    On, officer, to prison till it come.

[*Exeunt* SECOND MERCHANT, ANGELO, OFFICER, *and*
ANTIPHOLUS *of Ephesus.*]

DROMIO OF SYRACUSE. To Adriana! that is where we dined,
    Where Dowsabel did claim me for her husband:
    She is too big, I hope, for me to compass.
    Thither I must, although against my will,
    For servants must their masters' minds fulfil. [*Exit.*]

SCENE II.

A Room in the House of ANTIPHOLUS *of Ephesus.*

[*Enter* ADRIANA *and* LUCIANA.]

ADRIANA. Ah, Luciana, did he tempt thee so?
    Mightst thou perceive austerely in his eye
    That he did plead in earnest? yea or no?
    Look'd he or red or pale, or sad or merrily?
    What observation madest thou in this case
    Of his heart's meteors tilting in his face?[107]

---

[106] *Waftage* is *passage by water* or *on the waves.*—*Hire* is here a dissyllable; spelt
hier in the original. So *hour*, a little before in this scene: "I gave't you half an *hour*
since."

[107] *Meteors* here probably refers to the Aurora Borealis, which sometimes has the
appearance of armies meeting in battle. So in *Paradise Lost*, ii. 533:

LUCIANA. First he denied you had in him no right.[108]
ADRIANA. He meant he did me none; the more my spite.
LUCIANA. Then swore he that he was a stranger here.
ADRIANA. And true he swore, though yet forsworn he were.
LUCIANA. Then pleaded I for you.
ADRIANA. And what said he?
LUCIANA. That love I begg'd for you he begg'd of me.
ADRIANA. With what persuasion did he tempt thy love?
LUCIANA. With words that in an honest suit might move.
    First he did praise my beauty, then my speech.
ADRIANA. Didst speak him fair?
LUCIANA. Have patience, I beseech.
ADRIANA. I cannot, nor I will not, hold me still;
    My tongue, though not my heart, shall have his will.
    He is deformed, crooked, old and sere,[109]
    Ill-faced, worse bodied, shapeless everywhere;
    Vicious, ungentle, foolish, blunt, unkind;
    Stigmatical in making,[110] worse in mind.
LUCIANA. Who would be jealous then of such a one?
    No evil lost is wail'd when it is gone.
ADRIANA. Ah, but I think him better than I say,
    And yet would herein others' eyes were worse.
    Far from her nest the lapwing cries away:[111]
    My heart prays for him, though my tongue do curse.

[*Enter* DROMIO *of Syracuse.*]

DROMIO OF SYRACUSE. Here! go; the desk, the purse! sweet, now,
    make haste.
LUCIANA. How hast thou lost thy breath?
DROMIO OF SYRACUSE. By running fast.

    As when, to warn proud cities, war appears
    Waged in the troubled sky, and armies rush
    To battle in the clouds, before each van
    Prick forth the aëry knights, and couch their spears,
    Till thickest legions close.

[108] This double negative had the force of a strong affirmative. So in *King Richard the Third*, i. 3: "You may *deny* that you were *not* the cause of my Lord Hastings' late imprisonment."

[109] *Sere* is *dry, withered, in decay.* So in *Macbeth*, v. 3: "My way of life is fall'n into the *sere*, the *yellow* leaf."

[110] That is, *marked* by Nature with ugliness, or having a *stigma*, or note of disgrace, set upon it.

[111] This was a common proverbial saying. So in Lyly's *Alexander and Campaspe:* "You resemble the lapwing, who cryeth most where her nest is not; and so, to lead me from espying your love for Campaspe, you cry Timoclea."

ADRIANA. Where is thy master, Dromio? is he well?

DROMIO OF SYRACUSE. No, he's in Tartar limbo, worse than Hell.
A Devil in an everlasting garment[112] hath him;
One whose hard heart is button'd up with steel;
A fiend, a fury, pitiless and rough;
A wolf, nay, worse,—a fellow all in buff;
A back-friend, a shoulder-clapper, one that countermands
The passages of alleys, creeks and narrow lands;
A hound that runs counter and yet draws dryfoot well;[113]
One that before the judgement carries poor souls to Hell.[114]

ADRIANA. Why, man, what is the matter?

DROMIO OF SYRACUSE. I do not know the matter: he is 'rested on the case.

ADRIANA. What, is he arrested? Tell me at whose suit.

DROMIO OF SYRACUSE. I know not at whose suit he is arrested well;
But he's in a suit of buff which 'rested him, that can I tell.
Will you send him, mistress, redemption, the money in his desk?

ADRIANA. Go fetch it, sister.—[*Exit* LUCIANA.]
This I wonder at,
That he, unknown to me, should be in debt.—
Tell me, was he arrested on a band?[115]

DROMIO OF SYRACUSE. Not on a band, but on a stronger thing,—
A chain, a chain! Do you not hear it ring?

ADRIANA. What, the chain?

DROMIO OF SYRACUSE. No, no, the bell: 'tis time that I were gone:
It was two ere I left him, and now the clock strikes one.

ADRIANA. The hours come back! that did I never hear.

DROMIO OF SYRACUSE. O, yes; if any hour[116] meet a sergeant, 'a

---

[112] The serjeant's *buff* or *leather* jerkin is called an "everlasting garment," probably because of its durability. So in *Henry IV., Part 1*, i. 2: "Is not a *buff jerkin* a most sweet robe of *durance?*"

[113] To *run counter* and to *draw dry foot* were terms of the chase. The latter was used of a hound that traced the game by the mere scent of the foot; as an animal running- over *dry* ground would naturally leave no *visible* footprints. To *run* or *hunt counter* was to course the trail backward, mistaking the direction of the game. A hound that *ran counter* was not likely to *draw dry foot well;* but the two things thus hardly compatible in themselves are here tied together by a quibble upon *counter,* which was the name of one of the London prisons. A sheriff's officer might be said to run counter, inasmuch as he took rogues to the Counter; and he might also be said to draw dry foot well, because the rogues whom he hunted were apt to have their purses empty, or *dry of cash.*

[114] Quibbles, again, both on *judgment* and on *Hell;* the former referring both to the Judgment-day, and to the sentence, *before* which the accused was held in prison for trial. *Hell* was a cant term for the worst dungeon in the prisons of the time.

[115] *Band* is an old spelling of *bond,* and has to be retained here on account of the quibble.

[116] From this, it seems probable that, as Mr. White observes, *hour* and *whore* were pronounced alike, or nearly so,—*hoor.*

turns back for very fear.

ADRIANA. As if Time were in debt! how fondly dost thou reason![117]

DROMIO OF SYRACUSE. Time is a very bankrupt, and owes more
than he's worth, to season.
Nay, he's a thief too: have you not heard men say
That Time comes stealing on by night and day?
If Time be in debt and theft, and a sergeant in the way,
Hath he not reason to turn back an hour in a day?

[*Re-enter* LUCIANA *with the purse.*]

ADRIANA. Go, Dromio; there's the money, bear it straight;
And bring thy master home immediately.
Come, sister: I am press'd down with conceit,[118]—
Conceit, my comfort and my injury. [*Exeunt.*]

SCENE III.

A public Place.

[*Enter* ANTIPHOLUS *of Syracuse.*]

ANTIPHOLUS OF SYRACUSE. There's not a man I meet but doth
salute me
As if I were their well-acquainted friend;
And every one doth call me by my name.
Some tender money to me; some invite me;
Some other give me thanks for kindnesses;
Some offer me commodities to buy:
Even now a tailor call'd me in[119] his shop
And show'd me silks that he had bought for me,
And therewithal took measure of my body.
Sure, these are but imaginary wiles
And Lapland sorcerers inhabit here.

[*Enter* DROMIO *of Syracuse.*]

DROMIO OF SYRACUSE. Master, here's the gold you sent me for.
What, have you got the picture of old Adam new-apparell'd?[120]

---

[117] To *talk* or *converse* is among the old senses of to *reason.*

[118] *Conceit* was always used in a good sense, that of *conception, imagination,* or *thought.*

[119] *In* and *into* were used interchangeably, at least to some extent.

[120] Singer's explanation of this queer passage is probably right: "The sergeant is designated by *the picture of old Adam*, because he wore buff, as Adam wore his native

ANTIPHOLUS OF SYRACUSE. What gold is this? what Adam dost thou mean?

DROMIO OF SYRACUSE. Not that Adam that kept the Paradise but that Adam that keeps the prison: he that goes in the calf's skin that was killed for the Prodigal; he that came behind you, sir, like an evil angel, and bid you forsake your liberty.

ANTIPHOLUS OF SYRACUSE. I understand thee not.

DROMIO OF SYRACUSE. No? why, 'tis a plain case: he that went, like a bass-viol, in a case of leather; the man, sir, that, when gentlemen are tired, gives them a bob,[121] and 'rests them; he, sir, that takes pity on decayed men and gives them suits of durance; he that sets up his rest[122] to do more exploits with his mace than a morris-pike.[123]

ANTIPHOLUS OF SYRACUSE. What, thou meanest an officer?

DROMIO OF SYRACUSE. Ay, sir, the sergeant of the band, he that brings any man to answer it that breaks his band; one that thinks a man always going to bed, and says, *God give you good rest*!

ANTIPHOLUS OF SYRACUSE. Well, sir, there rest in your foolery. Is there any ships put forth tonight? May we be gone?

DROMIO OF SYRACUSE. Why, sir, I brought you word an hour since that the bark Expedition put forth to-night; and then were you hindered by the sergeant, to tarry for the hoy *Delay*. Here are the angels[124] that you sent for to deliver you.

ANTIPHOLUS OF SYRACUSE. The fellow is distract,[125] and so am I;
And here we wander in illusions:
Some blessed power deliver us from hence!

[*Enter a* COURTEZAN.]

COURTEZAN. Well met, well met, Master Antipholus.
I see, sir, you have found the goldsmith now:
Is that the chain you promised me to-day?

---

buff; and Dromio asks Antipholus if he had *got* him *new-apparell'd*, that is, got him a new *suit*; in other words, got *rid* of him."

[121] *Bob* here means a *stroke* or *clap*. Dromio has already spoken of the sergeant as "a shoulder-clapper." The Poet elsewhere uses *bob* figuratively for *taunt* or *scoff*.

[122] *Setting up one's rest* is an old phrase for *resolving* or *making up one's mind* to do a thing. So in *The Merchant*, ii. 2, Launcelot quibbles upon it: "As I have *set up my rest* to run away, so I will not rest till I have run some ground." Also in *Romeo and Juliet*, iv. 5: "The County Paris hath *set up his rest*, that you shall rest but little."

[123] *Morris-pike* is a corruption of *Moorish pike*, the name of a weapon much used in the sixteenth century.

[124] *Angel* was the name of an English gold coin, worth about ten shillings. The Poet has many allusions to it. So in *The Merchant*, ii. 6: "They have in England a coin that bears the figure of an angel stamped in gold."

[125] *Distract* for *distracted*, just as, before, *ballast* for *ballasted*. Shakespeare has many such shortened preterites.

ANTIPHOLUS OF SYRACUSE. Satan, avoid! I charge thee, tempt me not.

DROMIO OF SYRACUSE. Master, is this Mistress Satan?

ANTIPHOLUS OF SYRACUSE. It is the Devil.

DROMIO OF SYRACUSE. Nay, she is worse, she is the Devil's dam; and here she comes in the habit of a light wench: and thereof comes that the wenches say, *God damn me*; that's as much to say *God make me a light wench.* It is written, they appear to men like angels of light: light is an effect of fire, and fire will burn; *ergo*, light wenches will burn. Come not near her.

COURTEZAN. Your man and you are marvellous merry, sir.
    Will you go with me? We'll mend our dinner here?

DROMIO OF SYRACUSE. Master, if you do, expect spoon-meat; or bespeak a long spoon.

ANTIPHOLUS OF SYRACUSE. Why, Dromio?

DROMIO OF SYRACUSE. Marry, he must have a long spoon that must eat with the Devil.[126]

ANTIPHOLUS OF SYRACUSE. Avoid then, fiend! what tell'st thou me of supping?
    Thou art, as you are all, a sorceress:
    I conjure thee to leave me and be gone.

COURTEZAN. Give me the ring of mine you had at dinner,
    Or, for my diamond, the chain you promised,
    And I'll be gone, sir, and not trouble you.

DROMIO OF SYRACUSE. Some devils ask but the parings of one's nail,
    A rush, a hair, a drop of blood, a pin,
    A nut, a cherry-stone;
    But she, more covetous, would have a chain.
    Master, be wise: an if you give it her,
    The Devil will shake her chain and fright us with it.

COURTEZAN. I pray you, sir, my ring, or else the chain:
    I hope you do not mean to cheat me so.

ANTIPHOLUS OF SYRACUSE. Avaunt, thou witch!—Come, Dromio, let us go.

DROMIO OF SYRACUSE. *Fly pride*, says the peacock: mistress, that you know.

[*Exeunt* ANTIPHOLUS *of Syracuse and* DROMIO *of Syracuse.*]

COURTEZAN. Now, out of doubt Antipholus is mad,
    Else would he never so demean himself.

---

[126] "He that eats with the Devil has need of a long spoon," is an old proverb. Referred to again in *The Tempest.*

A ring he hath of mine worth forty ducats,
And for the same he promised me a chain:
Both one and other he denies me now.
The reason that I gather he is mad,—
Besides this present instance of his rage,—
Is a mad tale he told to-day at dinner,
Of his own doors being shut against his entrance.
Belike his wife, acquainted with his fits,
On purpose shut the doors against his way.
My way is now to hie home to his house,
And tell his wife that, being lunatic,
He rush'd into my house and took perforce
My ring away. This course I fittest choose;
For forty ducats is too much to lose. [*Exit.*]

SCENE IV.

A Street.

[*Enter* ANTIPHOLUS *of Ephesus and the* OFFICER.]

ANTIPHOLUS OF EPHESUS. Fear me not, man; I will not break
away:
I'll give thee, ere I leave thee, so much money,
To warrant thee, as I am 'rested for.
My wife is in a wayward mood to-day,
And will not lightly trust the messenger
That I should be attach'd in Ephesus,
I tell you, 'twill sound harshly in her ears.
Here comes my man; I think he brings the money.—

[*Enter* DROMIO *of Ephesus with a rope's-end.*]

How now, sir! have you that I sent you for?
DROMIO OF EPHESUS. Here's that, I warrant you, will pay them all.
ANTIPHOLUS OF EPHESUS. But where's the money?
DROMIO OF EPHESUS. Why, sir, I gave the money for the rope.
ANTIPHOLUS OF EPHESUS. Five hundred ducats, villain, for a
rope?
DROMIO OF EPHESUS. I'll serve you, sir, five hundred at the rate.
ANTIPHOLUS OF EPHESUS. To what end did I bid thee hie thee
home?
DROMIO OF EPHESUS. To a rope's-end, sir; and to that end am I
returned.
ANTIPHOLUS OF EPHESUS. And to that end, sir, I will welcome

you.

[*Beating him.*]

OFFICER. Good sir, be patient.
DROMIO OF EPHESUS. Nay, 'tis for me to be patient; I am in adversity.
OFFICER. Good now,[127] hold thy tongue.
DROMIO OF EPHESUS. Nay, rather persuade him to hold his hands.
ANTIPHOLUS OF EPHESUS. Thou whoreson, senseless villain!
DROMIO OF EPHESUS. I would I were senseless, sir, that I might not feel your blows.
ANTIPHOLUS. Thou art sensible in[128] nothing but blows, and so is an ass.
DROMIO OF EPHESUS. I am an ass, indeed; you may prove it by my long 'ears.[129]—I have served him from the hour of my nativity to this instant, and have nothing at his hands for my service but blows. When I am cold, he heats me with beating; when I am warm, he cools me with beating; I am waked with it when I sleep; raised with it when I sit; driven out of doors with it when I go from home; welcomed home with it when I return; nay, I bear it on my shoulders, as a beggar wont her brat; and, I think when he hath lamed me, I shall beg with it from door to door.
ANTIPHOLUS OF EPHESUS. Come, go along; my wife is coming yonder.

[*Enter* ADRIANA, LUCIANA, *the* COURTEZAN, *and* PINCH.]

DROMIO OF EPHESUS. Mistress, *respice finem*, respect your end; or rather, the prophecy like the parrot,[130] *Beware the rope's-end.*
ANTIPHOLUS OF EPHESUS. Wilt thou still talk?

---

[127] Shakespeare has *good now* repeatedly with the exact meaning of *well now.* So in *hamlet*, i. 1: "*Good now*, sit down, and tell me, he that knows," &c.

[128] *Sensitive to* is the meaning. The Poet has *sensible* repeatedly, where we should use sensitive.

[129] A quibble between *ears* and *years*, which were probably sounded much alike, as they still are in some places. So, as the Cambridge Editors note, it appears from what follows.

[130] Parrots were specially taught unlucky words; and if any passer-by took offence at these, the owner was wont to say, "Take heed, sir, my parrot prophesies." So in *Hudibras*, referring to Ralpho's skill in augury:

> Could tell what subtlest parrots mean,
> That speak, and think contrary clean;
> What member 'tis of whom they talk,
> When they cry *rope*, and *walk, knave, walk.*

[Beating him.]

COURTEZAN. How say you now? is not your husband mad?
ADRIANA. His incivility confirms no less.
    Good Doctor Pinch, you are a conjurer;
    Establish him in his true sense again,
    And I will please you what you will demand.
LUCIANA. Alas, how fiery and how sharp he looks!
COURTEZAN. Mark how he trembles in his ecstasy![131]
PINCH. Give me your hand and let me feel your pulse.
ANTIPHOLUS OF EPHESUS. There is my hand, and let it feel your
    ear.

[Striking him.]

PINCH. I charge thee, Satan, housed within this man,
    To yield possession to my holy prayers
    And to thy state of darkness hie thee straight:
    I conjure thee by all the saints in Heaven!
ANTIPHOLUS OF EPHESUS. Peace, doting wizard, peace! I am not
    mad.
ADRIANA. O, that thou wert not, poor distressed soul!
ANTIPHOLUS OF EPHESUS. You minion, you, are these your
    customers?[132]
    Did this companion[133] with the saffron face
    Revel and feast it at my house to-day,
    Whilst upon me the guilty doors were shut
    And I denied to enter in my house?
ADRIANA. O husband, God doth know you dined at home;
    Where would you had remain'd until this time,
    Free from these slanders and this open shame!
ANTIPHOLUS OF EPHESUS. Dined at home!—Thou villain, what
    sayest thou?
DROMIO OF EPHESUS. Sir, sooth to say, you did not dine at home.
ANTIPHOLUS OF EPHESUS. Were not my doors lock'd up and I
    shut out?
DROMIO OF EPHESUS. Perdy,[134] your doors were lock'd and you

---

[131] This *tremor* was thought to be a sure sign of diabolical possession. In *The Tempest*, ii. 2, Caliban says, "Thou dost me yet but little hurt; thou wilt anon, I know it by thy *trembling.*"

[132] A *customer* was a *familiar*, one *accustomed to haunt any place.* So defined in old dictionaries.

[133] *Companion* was used as a word of contempt, as *fellow* is now.

[134] *Perdy* is an ancient corruption of *par Dieu.*

shut out.

ANTIPHOLUS OF EPHESUS. And did not she herself revile me there?

DROMIO OF EPHESUS. Sans fable, she herself reviled you there.

ANTIPHOLUS OF EPHESUS. Did not her kitchen-maid rail, taunt, and scorn me?

DROMIO OF EPHESUS. Certes, she did; the kitchen-vestal scorn'd you.

ANTIPHOLUS OF EPHESUS. And did not I in rage depart from thence?

DROMIO OF EPHESUS. In verity you did;—my bones bear witness,
That since have felt the vigour of his rage.

ADRIANA. Is't good to soothe him in these contraries?

PINCH. It is no shame: the fellow finds his vein,
And yielding to him humours well his frenzy.

ANTIPHOLUS OF EPHESUS. Thou hast suborn'd the goldsmith to arrest me.

ADRIANA. Alas, I sent you money to redeem you,
By Dromio here, who came in haste for it.

DROMIO OF EPHESUS. Money by me! heart and goodwill you might;
But surely master, not a rag of money.

ANTIPHOLUS OF EPHESUS. Went'st not thou to her for a purse of ducats?

ADRIANA. He came to me and I deliver'd it.

LUCIANA. And I am witness with her that she did.

DROMIO OF EPHESUS. God and the rope-maker bear me witness
That I was sent for nothing but a rope!

PINCH. Mistress, both man and master is possess'd;
I know it by their pale and deadly looks:
They must be bound and laid in some dark room.

ANTIPHOLUS OF EPHESUS. [*To* ADRIANA.] Say, wherefore didst thou lock me forth to-day?
And why dost thou deny the bag of gold?

ADRIANA. I did not, gentle husband, lock thee forth.

DROMIO OF EPHESUS. And, gentle master, I received no gold;
But I confess, sir, that we were lock'd out.

ADRIANA. Dissembling villain, thou speak'st false in both.

ANTIPHOLUS OF EPHESUS. Dissembling harlot, thou art false in all;
And art confederate with a damned pack
To make a loathsome abject scorn of me:
But with these nails I'll pluck out these false eyes
That would behold in me this shameful sport.

ADRIANA. O, bind him, bind him! let him not come near me.

PINCH. More company! The fiend is strong within him.
LUCIANA. Ay me, poor man, how pale and wan he looks!

[*Enter three or four, who assist* PINCH *in binding him.*]

ANTIPHOLUS OF EPHESUS. What, will you murder me?—Thou
      Jailer, thou,
  I am thy prisoner: wilt thou suffer them
  To make a rescue?
OFFICER. Masters, let him go
  He is my prisoner, and you shall not have him.
PINCH. Go bind this man, for he is frantic too.
ADRIANA. What wilt thou do, thou peevish officer?
  Hast thou delight to see a wretched man
  Do outrage and displeasure to himself?
OFFICER. He is my prisoner: if I let him go,
  The debt he owes will be required of me.
ADRIANA. I will discharge thee ere I go from thee:
  Bear me forthwith unto his creditor,
  And, knowing how the debt grows, I will pay it.—
  Good master doctor, see him safe convey'd
  Home to my house. O most unhappy[135] day!
ANTIPHOLUS OF EPHESUS. O most unhappy strumpet!
DROMIO OF EPHESUS. Master, I am here entered in bond for you.
ANTIPHOLUS OF EPHESUS. Out on thee, villain! wherefore dost
      thou mad me?
DROMIO OF EPHESUS. Will you be bound for nothing? be mad,
      good master: cry 'The Devil!'
LUCIANA. God help, poor souls, how idly do they talk!
ADRIANA. Go bear him hence. Sister, go you with me.

[*Exeunt* PINCH *and* Assistants *with* ANTIPHOLUS *of Ephesus,
    and* DROMIO *of Ephesus.*]

  Say now, whose suit is he arrested at?
OFFICER. One Angelo, a goldsmith: do you know him?
ADRIANA. I know the man. What is the sum he owes?
OFFICER. Two hundred ducats.
ADRIANA. Say, how grows it due?
OFFICER. Due for a chain your husband had of him.
ADRIANA. He did bespeak a chain for me, but had it not.
COURTEZAN. When as your husband all in rage to-day

---

[135] *Unhappy* here is *mischievous*, that which *causes ill hap;* like the Latin *infelix.*
The Poet has it repeatedly so.

Came to my house and took away my ring,—
The ring I saw upon his finger now,—
Straight after did I meet him with a chain.
ADRIANA. It may be so, but I did never see it.—
Come, Jailer, bring me where the goldsmith is:
I long to know the truth hereof at large.

[*Enter* ANTIPHOLUS *of Syracuse and* DROMIO *of Syracuse with their rapiers drawn.*]

LUCIANA. God, for thy mercy! they are loose again.
ADRIANA. And come with naked swords.
Let's call more help to have them bound again.
OFFICER. Away! they'll kill us.

[*Exeunt* ADRIANA, LUCIANA, *the* Courtezan, *and* Officer.]

ANTIPHOLUS OF SYRACUSE. I see these witches are afraid of swords.
DROMIO OF SYRACUSE. She that would be your wife now ran from you.
ANTIPHOLUS OF SYRACUSE. Come to the Centaur; fetch our stuff[136] from thence:
I long that we were safe and sound aboard.
DROMIO OF SYRACUSE. Faith, stay here this night; they will surely do us no harm: you saw they speak us fair, give us gold: methinks they are such a gentle nation that, but for the mountain of mad flesh that claims marriage of me, I could find in my heart to stay here still and turn witch.
ANTIPHOLUS OF SYRACUSE. I will not stay to-night for all the town;
Therefore away, to get our stuff aboard. [*Exeunt.*]

---

[136] *Stuff* here means *luggage* or *movables.* So in St. Luke, xvii. 31: "In that day, lie which shall be upon the house-top, and his *stuff* in the house, let him not come down to take it away."

Act V.

Scene I.

Before an Abbey.

[*Enter Second* MERCHANT *and* ANGELO.]

ANGELO. I am sorry, sir, that I have hinder'd you;
 But, I protest, he had the chain of me,
 Though most dishonestly he doth deny it.
SECOND MERCHANT. How is the man esteemed here in the city?
ANGELO. Of very reverend reputation, sir,
 Of credit infinite, highly beloved,
 Second to none that lives here in the city:
 His word might bear my wealth at any time.
SECOND MERCHANT. Speak softly; yonder, as I think, he walks.

[*Enter* ANTIPHOLUS *of Syracuse and* DROMIO *of Syracuse.*]

ANGELO. 'Tis so; and that self chain about his neck
 Which he forswore most monstrously to have.
 Good sir, draw near to me, I'll speak to him.—
 Signior Antipholus, I wonder much
 That you would put me to this shame and trouble;
 And, not without some scandal to yourself,
 With circumstance and oaths so to deny
 This chain which now you wear so openly:
 Beside the charge, the shame, imprisonment,
 You have done wrong to this my honest friend,
 Who, but for staying on our controversy,
 Had hoisted sail and put to sea to-day:
 This chain you had of me; can you deny it?
ANTIPHOLUS OF SYRACUSE. I think I had; I never did deny it.
SECOND MERCHANT. Yes, that you did, sir, and forswore it too.
ANTIPHOLUS OF SYRACUSE. Who heard me to deny it or forswear
 it?
SECOND MERCHANT. These ears of mine, thou know'st did hear
  thee.
 Fie on thee, wretch! 'tis pity that thou livest
 To walk where any honest man resort.
ANTIPHOLUS OF SYRACUSE. Thou art a villain to impeach me
  thus:
 I'll prove mine honour and mine honesty

Against thee presently, if thou darest stand.
SECOND MERCHANT. I dare, and do defy thee for a villain.

[*They draw.*]

[*Enter* ADRIANA, LUCIANA, *the* Courtezan, *and others.*]

ADRIANA. Hold, hurt him not, for God's sake! he is mad.
  Some get within him,[137] take his sword away:
  Bind Dromio too, and bear them to my house.
DROMIO OF SYRACUSE. Run, master, run; for God's sake, take a
    house![138]
  This is some priory. In, or we are spoil'd!

[*Exeunt* ANTIPHOLUS *of Syracuse and* DROMIO *of Syracuse
  into the abbey.*]

[*Enter the* ABBESS.]

ABBESS. Be quiet, people. Wherefore throng you hither?
ADRIANA. To fetch my poor distracted husband hence.
  Let us come in, that we may bind him fast
  And bear him home for his recovery.
ANGELO. I knew he was not in his perfect wits.
SECOND MERCHANT. I am sorry now that I did draw on him.
ABBESS. How long hath this possession held the man?
ADRIANA. This week he hath been heavy, sour,[139] sad,
  And much different from the man he was;
  But till this afternoon his passion
  Ne'er brake into extremity of rage.
ABBESS. Hath he not lost much wealth by wreck of sea?
  Buried some dear friend? Hath not else his eye
  Stray'd[140] his affection in unlawful love,—
  A sin prevailing much in youthful men,
  Who give their eyes the liberty of gazing.
  Which of these sorrows is he subject to?
ADRIANA. To none of these, except it be the last;
  Namely, some love that drew him oft from home.
ABBESS. You should for that have reprehended him.
ADRIANA. Why, so I did.

---

[137] Get *inside of his blows;* that is, *grapple with him.*

[138] As we still say *take refuge,* and *take sanctuary.*

[139] *Sour* is here a dissyllable, as *hour* and *hire* before.

[140] *Stray'd* is here a causative verb, meaning *misled,* or *made to stray;* a singular use of the word.

ABBESS. Ay, but not rough enough.

ADRIANA. As roughly as my modesty would let me.

ABBESS. Haply, in private.

ADRIANA. And in assemblies too.

ABBESS. Ay, but not enough.

ADRIANA. It was the copy of our conference:[141]
 In bed he slept not for my urging it;
 At board he fed not for my urging it;
 Alone, it was the subject of my theme;
 In company I often glanced it;
 Still did I tell him it was vile and bad.

ABBESS. And thereof came it that the man was mad.
 The venom clamours of a jealous woman
 Poisons more deadly than a mad dog's tooth.
 It seems his sleeps were hinder'd by thy railing,
 And therefore comes it that his head is light.
 Thou say'st his meat was sauced with thy upbraidings:
 Unquiet meals make ill digestions;—
 Thereof the raging fire of fever bred;
 And what's a fever but a fit of madness?
 Thou say'st his sports were hinderd by thy brawls:
 Sweet recreation barr'd, what doth ensue
 But moody and dull melancholy,
 Kinsman to grim and comfortless despair,
 And at her[142] heels a huge infectious troop
 Of pale distemperatures and foes to life?
 In food, in sport and life-preserving rest
 To be disturb'd, would mad or man or beast:
 The consequence is then thy jealous fits
 Have scared thy husband from the use of wits.

LUCIANA. She never reprehended him but mildly,
 When he demean'd himself rough, rude and wildly.—
 Why bear you these rebukes and answer not?

ADRIANA. She did betray me to my own reproof.—
 Good people enter and lay hold on him.

ABBESS. No, not a creature enters in my house.

ADRIANA. Then let your servants bring my husband forth.

ABBESS. Neither: he took this place for sanctuary,
 And it shall privilege him from your hands

---

[141] *Copy* here seems to mean *principal topic* or *theme;* that is, the *pattern* or *form* after which the conversation was shaped.

[142] *Her,* referring to *kinsman,* sounds rather ajar; but *kinsman* has merely the sense of *akin.* The Poet elsewhere indulges a like confusion of genders; as in *The Merchant,* iii. 2: "But now I was the *lord* of this fair mansion, *master* o'er my servants, *queen* o'er myself."

    Till I have brought him to his wits again,
    Or lose my labour in assaying it.
ADRIANA. I will attend my husband, be his nurse,
    Diet his sickness, for it is my office,
    And will have no attorney but myself;
    And therefore let me have him home with me.
ABBESS. Be patient; for I will not let him stir
    Till I have used the approved means I have,
    With wholesome syrups, drugs and holy prayers,
    To make of him a formal man[143] again:
    It is a branch and parcel of mine oath,
    A charitable duty of my order.
    Therefore depart and leave him here with me.
ADRIANA. I will not hence and leave my husband here:
    And ill it doth beseem your holiness
    To separate the husband and the wife.
ABBESS. Be quiet and depart: thou shalt not have him. [*Exit.*]
LUCIANA. Complain unto the duke of this indignity.
ADRIANA. Come, go: I will fall prostrate at his feet
    And never rise until my tears and prayers
    Have won his grace to come in person hither
    And take perforce my husband from the abbess.
SECOND MERCHANT. By this, I think, the dial points at five:
    Anon, I'm sure, the duke himself in person
    Comes this way to the melancholy vale,
    The place of death and sorry execution,
    Behind the ditches of the abbey here.
ANGELO. Upon what cause?
SECOND MERCHANT. To see a reverend Syracusian merchant,
    Who put unluckily into this bay
    Against the laws and statutes of this town,
    Beheaded publicly for his offence.
ANGELO. See where they come: we will behold his death.
LUCIANA. Kneel to the duke before he pass the abbey.

    [*Enter the* DUKE, *attended*; ÆGEON *bareheaded*; *with the*
    Headsman *and other* OFFICERS.]

DUKE SOLINUS. Yet once again proclaim it publicly,
    If any friend will pay the sum for him,
    He shall not die; so much we tender him.
ADRIANA. Justice, most sacred duke, against the abbess!
DUKE SOLINUS. She is a virtuous and a reverend lady:

---

[143] A *formal* man is a *rational* man, one whose mind is in *due form.*

It cannot be that she hath done thee wrong.

ADRIANA. May it please your grace, Antipholus, my husband,—
 Whom I made lord of me and all I had,
 At your important[144] letters,—this ill day
 A most outrageous fit of madness took him;
 That desperately he hurried through the street,—
 With him his bondman, all as mad as he—
 Doing displeasure to the citizens
 By rushing in their houses, bearing thence
 Rings, jewels, any thing his rage did like.
 Once did I get him bound and sent him home,
 Whilst to take order[145] for the wrongs I went,
 That here and there his fury had committed.
 Anon, I wot not by what strong escape,
 He broke from those that had the guard of him;
 And with his mad attendant and himself,
 Each one with ireful passion, with drawn swords,
 Met us again and madly bent on us,
 Chased us away; till, raising of more aid,
 We came again to bind them. Then they fled
 Into this abbey, whither we pursued them:
 And here the abbess shuts the gates on us
 And will not suffer us to fetch him out,
 Nor send him forth that we may bear him hence.
 Therefore, most gracious duke, with thy command
 Let him be brought forth and borne hence for help.

DUKE SOLINUS. Long since thy husband served me in my wars,
 And I to thee engaged a prince's word,
 When thou didst make him master of thy bed,
 To do him all the grace and good I could.—
 Go, some of you, knock at the abbey-gate
 And bid the lady abbess come to me.—
 I will determine this before I stir.

[*Enter a* SERVANT.]

---

[144] *Important* for *importunate.* So in *King Lear*, iv. 4: "Therefore great France my mourning and *important* tears hath pitied."—Upon the passage in the text, Malone notes as follows: "Shakespeare was thinking particularly on the interest which the king had in England in the marriage of his wards; who were the heirs of his tenants holding by knight's service, or *in capite*, and were under age;—an interest which Queen Elizabeth exerted on all occasions, as did her successors, till the abolition of the Court of Wards and Liveries. The Poet attributes to the Duke the same right to choose a wife or a husband for his wards at Ephesus."

[145] "Take order" is the old phrase for take *measures*, or make arrangements. Shakespeare has it repeatedly so.

SERVANT. O mistress, mistress, shift and save yourself!
    My master and his man are both broke loose,
    Beaten the maids a-row,[146] and bound the doctor
    Whose beard they have singed off with brands of fire;
    And ever, as it blazed, they threw on him
    Great pails of puddled mire to quench the hair:
    My master preaches patience to him and the while
    His man with scissors nicks him like a fool;[147]
    And sure, unless you send some present help,
    Between them they will kill the conjurer.
ADRIANA. Peace, fool! thy master and his man are here,
    And that is false thou dost report to us.
SERVANT. Mistress, upon my life, I tell you true;
    I have not breathed almost since I did see it.
    He cries for you, and vows, if he can take you,
    To scotch[148] your face and to disfigure you. [*Cry within.*]
    Hark, hark! I hear him, mistress. fly, be gone!
DUKE SOLINUS. Come, stand by me; fear nothing.—Guard with
    halberds!
ADRIANA. Ay me, it is my husband! Witness you,
    That he is borne about invisible:
    Even now we housed him in the abbey here;
    And now he's there, past thought of human reason.

[*Enter* ANTIPHOLUS *of Ephesus and* DROMIO *of Ephesus.*]

ANTIPHOLUS OF EPHESUS. Justice, most gracious duke, O, grant
    me justice!
    Even for the service that long since I did thee,
    When I bestrid thee[149] in the wars and took
    Deep scars to save thy life; even for the blood
    That then I lost for thee, now grant me justice.
ÆGEON. Unless the fear of death doth make me dote,
    I see my son Antipholus and Dromio.
ANTIPHOLUS OF EPHESUS. Justice, sweet prince, against that
    woman there!
    She whom thou gavest to me to be my wife,

---

[146] *A-row* is *in succession* or *one after another.*

[147] The hair of fools was cut into *notches* or *nicks.* So in *The Choice of Change,* 1598: "Three things used by monks which provoke other men to laugh at their follies, 1. They are shaven and *notched* on the head *like fooles.*"

[148] To *scotch* is to *score* or *cut slightly.* So in *Macbeth,* iii. 2: "We have but *scotch'd* the snake, not kill'd it."

[149] To *bestride* one when down in battle was considered a high act of service. So, in *Henry IV., Part 1,* v. 1, Falstaff says to the Prince, "Hal, if thou see me down in the battle, and *bestride me,* so; 'tis a point of friendship."

That hath abused and dishonour'd me
Even in the strength and height of injury!
Beyond imagination is the wrong
That she this day hath shameless thrown on me.
DUKE SOLINUS. Discover how, and thou shalt find me just.
ANTIPHOLUS OF EPHESUS. This day, great duke, she shut the doors
    upon me,
While she with harlots[150] feasted in my house.
DUKE SOLINUS. A grievous fault!—Say, woman, didst thou so?
ADRIANA. No, my good lord: myself, he and my sister
    To-day did dine together. So befall my soul
    As this is false he burdens me withal!
LUCIANA. Ne'er may I look on day, nor sleep on night,
    But she tells to your highness simple truth!
ANGELO. O perjured woman!—They are both forsworn:
    In this the madman justly chargeth them.
ANTIPHOLUS OF EPHESUS. My liege, I am advised[151] what I say,
    Neither disturbed with the effect of wine,
    Nor heady-rash, provoked with raging ire,
    Albeit my wrongs might make one wiser mad.
    This woman lock'd me out this day from dinner:
    That goldsmith there, were he not pack'd[152] with her,
    Could witness it, for he was with me then;
    Who parted with me to go fetch a chain,
    Promising to bring it to the Porpentine,
    Where Balthazar and I did dine together.
    Our dinner done, and he not coming thither,
    I went to seek him: in the street I met him
    And in his company that gentleman.

[Points to the Second MERCHANT.]

    There did this perjured goldsmith swear me down
    That I this day of him received the chain,
    Which, God he knows, I saw not: for the which
    He did arrest me with an officer.
    I did obey, and sent my peasant home
    For certain ducats: he with none return'd
    Then fairly I bespoke the officer
    To go in person with me to my house.

---

[150] *Harlot* was formerly a general term of reproach, applied to certain descriptions of men, as well as to loose women.

[151] *Advised*, here, is *circumspect, considerate*, or *calmly assured of.* Repeatedly thus.

[152] *Pack'd* is *leagued* or *confederate. Pact* is still used for *agreement* or *compact.*

By the way we met
My wife, her sister, and a rabble more
Of vile confederates. Along with them
They brought one Pinch, a hungry lean-faced villain,
A mere anatomy, a mountebank,
A threadbare juggler and a fortune-teller,
A needy, hollow-eyed, sharp-looking wretch,
A dead-looking man: this pernicious slave,
Forsooth, took on him as a conjurer,
And, gazing in mine eyes, feeling my pulse,
And with no face, as 'twere, outfacing me,
Cries out, I was possess'd. Then all together
They fell upon me, bound me, bore me thence
And in a dark and dankish vault at home
There left me and my man, both bound together;
Till, gnawing with my teeth my bonds in sunder,
I gain'd my freedom, and immediately
Ran hither to your grace; whom I beseech
To give me ample satisfaction
For these deep shames and great indignities.
ANGELO. My lord, in truth, thus far I witness with him,
That he dined not at home, but was lock'd out.
DUKE SOLINUS. But had he such a chain of thee or no?
ANGELO. He had, my lord: and when he ran in here,
These people saw the chain about his neck.
SECOND MERCHANT. Besides, I will be sworn these ears of mine
Heard you confess you had the chain of him
After you first forswore it on the mart:
And thereupon I drew my sword on you;
And then you fled into this abbey here,
From whence, I think, you are come by miracle.
ANTIPHOLUS OF EPHESUS. I never came within these abbey-walls,
Nor ever didst thou draw thy sword on me:
I never saw the chain, so help me Heaven!
And this is false you burden me withal.
DUKE SOLINUS. Why, what an intricate impeach[153] is this!
I think you all have drunk of Circe's cup.
If here you housed him, here he would have been;
If he were mad, he would not plead so coldly:—
You say he dined at home; the goldsmith here
Denies that saying.—Sirrah, what say you?
DROMIO OF EPHESUS. Sir, he dined with her there, at the

---

[153] *Impeach* for *impeachment*, that is, *accusation*. So the Poet has *suspect* for *suspicion* repeatedly; and *dispose* for *disposal* or *disposition*.

Porpentine.

COURTEZAN. He did, and from my finger snatch'd that ring.

ANTIPHOLUS OF EPHESUS. 'Tis true, my liege; this ring I had of
  her.

DUKE SOLINUS. Saw'st thou him enter at the abbey here?

COURTEZAN. As sure, my liege, as I do see your grace.

DUKE SOLINUS. Why, this is strange.—Go call the abbess hither.—

[*Exit an* ATTENDANT.]

I think you are all mated[154] or stark mad.

ÆGEON. Most mighty duke, vouchsafe me speak a word:
  Haply I see a friend will save my life
  And pay the sum that may deliver me.

DUKE SOLINUS. Speak freely, Syracusian, what thou wilt.

ÆGEON. Is not your name, sir, call'd Antipholus?
  And is not that your bondman, Dromio?

DROMIO OF EPHESUS. Within this hour I was his bondman sir,
  But he, I thank him, gnaw'd in two my cords:
  Now am I Dromio and his man unbound.

ÆGEON. I am sure you both of you remember me.

DROMIO OF EPHESUS. Ourselves we do remember, sir, by you;
  For lately we were bound, as you are now
  You are not Pinch's patient, are you, sir?

ÆGEON. Why look you strange on me? you know me well.

ANTIPHOLUS. I never saw you in my life till now.

ÆGEON. O, grief hath changed me since you saw me last,
  And careful hours with time's deformed[155] hand
  Have written strange defeatures in my face:
  But tell me yet, dost thou not know my voice?

ANTIPHOLUS OF EPHESUS. Neither.

ÆGEON. Dromio, nor thou?

DROMIO OF EPHESUS. No, trust me, sir, nor I.

ÆGEON. I am sure thou dost.

DROMIO OF EPHESUS. Ay, sir, but I am sure I do not; and
  whatsoever a man denies, you are now bound to believe him.

ÆGEON. Not know my voice! O time's extremity,
  Hast thou so crack'd and splitted my poor tongue
  In seven short years, that here my only son
  Knows not my feeble key of untuned cares?
  Though now this grained face of mine be hid

---

[154] *Mated* is *confounded* or *bewildered.* See page 35, note 88.
[155] *Deformed* for *deforming;* the active and passive forms being then often used
interchangeably.

In sap-consuming winter's drizzled snow,
And all the conduits of my blood froze up,
Yet hath my night of life some memory,
My wasting lamps some fading glimmer left,
My dull deaf ears a little use to hear:
All these old witnesses—I cannot err—
Tell me thou art my son Antipholus.
ANTIPHOLUS OF EPHESUS. I never saw my father in my life.
ÆGEON. But seven years since, in Syracusa, boy,
Thou know'st we parted: but perhaps, my son,
Thou shamest to acknowledge me in misery.
ANTIPHOLUS OF EPHESUS. The duke and all that know me in the
city
Can witness with me that it is not so
I ne'er saw Syracusa in my life.
DUKE SOLINUS. I tell thee, Syracusian, twenty years
Have I been patron to Antipholus,
During which time he ne'er saw Syracusa:
I see thy age and dangers make thee dote.

[*Re-enter the* ABBESS, *with* ANTIPHOLUS *of Syracuse and*
DROMIO *of Syracuse.*]

ABBESS. Most mighty duke, behold a man much wrong'd.

[*All gather to see them.*]

ADRIANA. I see two husbands, or mine eyes deceive me.
DUKE SOLINUS. One of these men is Genius to the other;
And so of these. Which is the natural man,
And which the spirit? who deciphers them?
DROMIO OF SYRACUSE. I, sir, am Dromio; command him away.
DROMIO OF EPHESUS. I, sir, am Dromio; pray, let me stay.
ANTIPHOLUS OF SYRACUSE. Ægeon art thou not? or else his
ghost?
DROMIO OF SYRACUSE. O, my old master! who hath bound him
here?
ABBESS. Whoever bound him, I will loose his bonds
And gain a husband by his liberty.—
Speak, old Ægeon, if thou be'st the man
That hadst a wife once call'd Æmilia
That bore thee at a burden two fair sons:
O, if thou be'st the same Ægeon, speak,
And speak unto the same Æmilia!
ÆGEON. If I dream not, thou art Æmilia:

If thou art she, tell me where is that son
That floated with thee on the fatal raft?

ABBESS. By men of Epidamnum he and I
And the twin Dromio all were taken up;
But by and by rude fishermen of Corinth
By force took Dromio and my son from them
And me they left with those of Epidamnum.
What then became of them I cannot tell
I to this fortune that you see me in.

DUKE SOLINUS. Why, here begins his morning story[156] right;
These two Antipholuses, these two so like,
And these two Dromios, one in semblance,—
Besides her urging of her wreck at sea,—
These are the parents to these children,
Which accidentally are met together.—
Antipholus, thou camest from Corinth first?

ANTIPHOLUS OF SYRACUSE. No, sir, not I; I came from Syracuse.

DUKE SOLINUS. Stay, stand apart; I know not which is which.

ANTIPHOLUS OF EPHESUS. I came from Corinth, my most gracious lord,—

DROMIO OF EPHESUS. And I with him.

ANTIPHOLUS OF EPHESUS.—Brought to this town by that most famous warrior,
Duke Menaphon, your most renowned uncle.

ADRIANA. Which of you two did dine with me to-day?

ANTIPHOLUS OF SYRACUSE. I, gentle mistress.

ADRIANA. And are not you my husband?

ANTIPHOLUS OF EPHESUS. No; I say nay to that.

ANTIPHOLUS OF SYRACUSE. And so do I; yet did she call me so:
And this fair gentlewoman, her sister here,
Did call me brother.—[*To* LUCIANA.] What I told you then,
I hope I shall have leisure to make good;
If this be not a dream I see and hear.

ANGELO. That is the chain, sir, which you had of me.

ANTIPHOLUS OF SYRACUSE. I think it be, sir; I deny it not.

ANTIPHOLUS OF EPHESUS. And you, sir, for this chain arrested me.

ANGELO. I think I did, sir; I deny it not.

ADRIANA. I sent you money, sir, to be your bail,
By Dromio; but I think he brought it not.

DROMIO OF EPHESUS. No, none by me.

ANTIPHOLUS OF SYRACUSE. This purse of ducats I received from you,
And Dromio, my man, did bring them me.

---

[156] The "morning story" is what Ægeon tells the Duke in the first scene of the play.

    I see we still did meet each other's man,
    And I was ta'en for him, and he for me,
    And thereupon these errors are arose.

ANTIPHOLUS OF EPHESUS. These ducats pawn I for my father here.

DUKE SOLINUS. It shall not need; thy father hath his life.

COURTEZAN. Sir, I must have that diamond from you.

ANTIPHOLUS OF EPHESUS. There, take it; and much thanks for my good cheer.

ABBESS. Renowned duke, vouchsafe to take the pains
    To go with us into the abbey here
    And hear at large discoursed all our fortunes;—
    And all that are assembled in this place,
    That by this sympathized one day's error
    Have suffer'd wrong, go keep us company,
    And we shall make full satisfaction.—
    Thirty-three years have I but gone in travail
    Of you, my sons; and till this present hour
    My heavy burden ne'er delivered.—
    The duke, my husband and my children both,
    And you the calendars of their nativity,[157]
    Go to a gossips' feast,[158] and go with me;
    After so long grief, such festivity!

DUKE SOLINUS. With all my heart, I'll gossip at this feast.

[*Exeunt the* DUKE, ABBESS, ÆGEON, COURTEZAN, *Second* MERCHANT, ANGELO, *and* ATTENDANTS.]

DROMIO OF SYRACUSE. Master, shall I fetch your stuff from shipboard?

ANTIPHOLUS OF EPHESUS. Dromio, what stuff of mine hast thou embark'd?

DROMIO OF SYRACUSE. Your goods that lay at host, sir, in the Centaur.

ANTIPHOLUS OF SYRACUSE. He speaks to me.—I am your master, Dromio:
    Come, go with us; we'll look to that anon:
    Embrace thy brother there; rejoice with him.

---

    [157] The two Dromios are called the calendars of their masters' nativity because they were born the same day. See page 15, note 25.

    [158] "A *gossips'* feast" is, literally, a feast of *sponsors; gossip* being from *God sib,* and *sib* meaning *kin.* Sponsors were wont to have a merry feast together after answering at the Font; and such feasts were apt occasions for *gossipping* in our sense of the term. The word is used here because Æmilia has just spoken of her sons as newly born, which implied them to be candidates for baptism.

[*Exeunt* ANTIPHOLUS *of Syracuse and* ANTIPHOLUS *of Ephesus.,* ADRIANA and LUCIANA.]

DROMIO OF SYRACUSE. There is a fat friend at your master's house,
  That kitchen'd me for you to-day at dinner:
  She now shall be my sister, not my wife.
DROMIO OF EPHESUS. Methinks you are my glass, and not my brother:
  I see by you I am a sweet-faced youth.
  Will you walk in to see their gossiping?
DROMIO OF SYRACUSE. Not I, sir; you are my elder.
DROMIO OF EPHESUS. That's a question: how shall we try it?
DROMIO OF SYRACUSE. We'll draw cuts for the senior: till then lead thou first.
DROMIO OF EPHESUS. Nay, then, thus:
  We came into the world like brother and brother;
  And now let's go hand in hand, not one before another. [*Exeunt.*]

THE END

Made in the USA
Middletown, DE
08 December 2019